PRESSURE COOKING
PROPERLY EXPLAINED

WITH RECIPES

PRESSURE COOKING PROPERLY EXPLAINED

WITH RECIPES

by
DIANNE PAGE

PAPERFRONTS

**ELLIOT RIGHT WAY BOOKS
KINGSWOOD, SURREY, U.K.**

Set, printed and bound in Great Britain by
Cox & Wyman Ltd, Reading

Contents

Illustrations

I

Introduction

If you have never used a pressure cooker before, or if your pressure cooker is languishing unused at the back of your kitchen cupboard, I hope you will find in this book a wide variety of recipes which will appeal to you and encourage you to try pressure cooking for yourself.

The old wives' tales about exploding pressure cookers are a relic of the past, as with today's safety-conscious designs, such incidents are extremely rare.

My first pressure cooker was a wedding present and after preparing two or three meals, carefully following instructions, I soon found that pressure cooking is straightforward and gives excellent results, quickly and conveniently.

Soon the pressure cooker became a way of life – just one more pan in the kitchen. The secret is to keep it handy as there is no truer saying than 'out of sight, out of mind'.

Pressure cooking is a good habit to get into and, I believe, an essential part of a busy life. I hope you will discover for yourself how the speed of pressure cooking can extend a busy cook's repertoire from homely everyday meals to more adventurous dinner party menus.

ADVANTAGES OF PRESSURE COOKING

Speed

People who have never used a pressure cooker before are often amazed at the short cooking times possible. Generally one can say that the time required for cooking under pressure is roughly one third that of conventional cooking. Some recipes save even more time. For example, an ordinary beef stew would normally take 1½ hours to cook, whereas in a pressure cooker it can be cooked in 15–20 minutes.

The speed of pressure cooking means that well-loved recipes, often neglected in the past because they need hours of cooking or close attention, can now be prepared quickly and easily. Some of these old favourites include Oxtail Soup, Steak and Kidney Pudding, Steamed Suet Pudding and Lemon Curd. Dried beans, which have again become popular, can also be cooked in a fraction of the normal time.

Fuel savings

Shorter cooking times mean that considerable fuel savings can be made. Remember too that once you have reached the required cooking pressure the heat is usually reduced to the minimum setting for the remaining time.

Even greater savings can be made if you cook more than one food in the pressure cooker at the same time. This is a great advantage to people living alone, possibly on a limited income, and Chapter 9 suggests some suitable menus.

Food costs

Savings don't stop with the reduced amount of fuel needed. A pressure cooker enables you to tenderise the cheaper cuts of meat which normally need long slow cooking to make them acceptable. Dried beans are a cheap source of protein and can be pressure cooked in 20 minutes.

Flavour, colour and nutrition

We all recognize the welcoming aroma of a tasty casserole bubbling away on the cooker but often forget that the flavour is also escaping with the steam. A pressure cooker is designed to trap most of the steam, in this way retaining most of the flavour.

Some food loses colour with long cooking so the speed of pressure cooking helps prevent this, particularly with vegetables.

No matter how food is cooked, a certain amount of nutritional value will be lost. Nevertheless, the shorter cooking in a pressure cooker, combined with the small quantity of liquid and absence of light and air, helps to retain vitamins and minerals which would normally be lost.

Less steam and reduced cooking smells

A pressure cooker allows only a small amount of steam to escape, which enables you to cook steamed puddings and stews without the windows running with condensation. Cooking smells in the kitchen are reduced for the same reason.

Freezer cooking

A pressure cooker can be used to cook in quantity for the freezer. It is well worthwhile to cook twice the amount you need and freeze half, as the extra preparation of ingredients takes a negligible time. Remember that by increasing the quantity of soup or stew it is not necessary to lengthen the pressure cooking time. The time is only increased if the bulk of a meat joint or a steamed pudding is greater. The main point to remember is not to over-fill the pressure cooker.

Diets

It is sometimes difficult to organize meals if one member of the family has to follow a special diet. A pressure cooker can tenderize meat, steam fish and cook special dishes in a very short time, so that a diet can be prepared quickly to coincide with the family's meal. You can use a pressure cooker to prepare baby foods; for example a meat and vegetable dish with an egg custard cooked at the same time.

Camping, caravans and boats

A pressure cooker is invaluable on holidays where time and space are at a premium, because it is so fast and can cook a complete meal. Families soon become tired of the 'fry-up' which characterizes most self-catering holidays, so a chance to cook a quick, filling casserole is very much appreciated.

WHAT IS PRESSURE COOKING?

When cooking in a saucepan, heat is lost as steam escapes from under the lid. A pressure cooker's lid fits so closely that an airtight seal is formed. This means that the steam is trapped and pressure can build up inside. When water boils in a saucepan it can't become hotter than boiling point, which is 100 degrees C. If water is heated under pressure it *is* possible to increase that temperature and therefore cook more quickly.

Generally, but not always, pressure cookers operate at three different pressures – 5 lb (low), 10 lb (medium) and 15 lb (high) pressure. At 5 lb (low) pressure water reaches 109 degrees C; at 10 lb (medium), 115 degrees C; and at 15 lb (high), 121 degrees C. As most food is usually pressure cooked at 15 lb (high) pressure, you can appreciate that the extra 21 degrees C help speed up cooking.

HOW TO CHOOSE A PRESSURE COOKER

All pressure cookers work on the basic principle described above. They do differ, however, in the way they operate. Some pressure cookers have a choice of three different pressures, for cooking different types of food, but some only cook at one fixed pressure.

If a pressure cooker has three pressures it is more versatile as it will cook a wider variety of food. For example, you would use 5 lb (low) pressure to cook a pudding containing a raising agent. This ensures that the pudding rises before it 'sets'. This pressure is also used for bottling fruit. When softening fruit for jam or jellies, 10 lb (medium) pressure is recommended. For everyday cooking of soups, vegetables and casserole type dishes, 15 lb (high) pressure is used.

Pressure cookers which work at a single fixed pressure tend to operate at a lower, rather than a higher, pressure. One such model on the market works only at $7\frac{1}{2}$ lb pressure. Cooking temperatures in this type of pressure cooker cannot reach as high as those in the first type of pressure cooker described. This means that cooking times are longer and recipes which recommend cooking at 15 lb (high) need twice the time when cooking at $7\frac{1}{2}$ lb pressure.

Before buying a pressure cooker you should decide which size you need. Even the smaller models will cook a stew for four people but would not be large enough for bulk cooking for the freezer or for fruit bottling. Bearing in mind that pressure cookers can last 20 to 25 years, newlyweds should consider the size they may need ten years hence when they may have a family. On the other hand, do not choose the biggest pressure cooker you can find if you don't cook in large quantities or are unlikely to bottle fruit. Don't forget, either, that you will need a convenient place to store it.

Most pressure cookers are made of aluminium which is lightweight and strong. It is ideal for cooking as it spreads heat quickly and evenly without 'hot spots' occurring. Make sure you choose a pressure cooker with a thick base because, as you will see later in the book, this base has to withstand sudden drops in temperature when it is taken hot from the cooker and stood in a bowl of cold water to reduce pressure. Without a sturdy base, in time, the bottom of the pressure cooker will bow and the pressure cooker won't work efficiently.

Fig. 1. Single (non-variable) pressure cooker.
This model operates at a single, non-variable pressure.

In some models, a clockwork timer activates an automatic pressure-reducing device after the chosen time, but do remember to switch off the heat immediately, otherwise the cooker would eventually boil dry!

Accessories vary from model to model but basically they all have a removable rack or trivet which is used to hold above the water level food which is to be steam cooked. This is necessary with vegetables, for example, especially if more than one type of vegetable is being cooked at the same

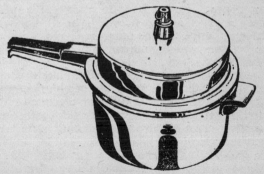

Fig. 2. Pressure cooker with variable pressures.
This pressure cooker operates at 5 lb, 10 lb, and 15 lb (low, medium and high) pressure.

time. Baskets are supplied to keep food apart so that the different flavours do not intermingle. The baskets are per-forated to allow the steam to circulate adequately. In some cases an unperforated basket is provided for cooking food such as egg custards, rice or stewed apple. A blanching basket can be bought separately and is very useful for blanching larger quantities of vegetables for freezing.

Don't have any fears about the safety of today's pressure cookers. Those made by reputable manufacturers are per-fectly safe to use and are fitted with devices which release pressure if the pressure cooker has been allowed to boil dry and over-heat. If you are in any doubt, look for a pressure cooker bearing the British Standards Kitemark of approval. This confirms that the pressure cooker is manufactured to their strict safety standards.

Fig. 3. Typical pressure cooker accessories.
Typical pressure cooker accessories include (left to right) unperforated basket, two perforated baskets, trivet and blanching basket.

When safety devices blow, it is often due to inadequate washing which leads to the air vents being blocked with stale food. Furthermore, if the lid is only half closed instead of being fully locked as instructed, the lid could fly off as pressure rises. These are obvious points but important none the less.

HOW TO USE A PRESSURE COOKER

Before using a pressure cooker for the first time, carefully read the manufacturer's instruction book. Different models vary and the book will tell you all you need to know about its operation. For those who have not yet acquired their own pressure cooker the following is a brief outline of how to use one.

A pressure cooker must contain a minimum amount of liquid to produce steam to raise pressure. The longer the cooking time, the greater the amount of liquid needed. Generally the minimum recommended by manufacturers for cooking times up to 30 minutes is 300ml ($\frac{1}{2}$ pint). This liquid can be water, stock, beer, cider, wine, soup, or made up of any combination of these. Oil cannot create steam and it would therefore be dangerous to cook using oil as the liquid. It is important to use the amount of liquid recommended for the recipe as too little could cause the pressure cooker to boil dry and overheat.

When cooking a soup or a casserole the trivet isn't needed as the flavours should intermingle during cooking. Some recipes require vegetables and meat to be sautéed in a little fat and this can be done in the open base of the pressure cooker before adding the liquid and remaining ingredients. If you need to use the trivet it is a good idea to put the water into the pressure cooker first. The water can't always be seen below the trivet and this way you avoid the risk of forgetting to add the liquid.

After adding the ingredients to the pressure cooker, the lid is fitted carefully. It is always important to ensure that the lid is tightly locked in position before allowing the pressure to rise. For pressure cookers with long, saucepan-type handles this means that the lid handle should lie directly over the base handle.

Once the lid is in position the pressure cooker can be brought to pressure. The way this is done depends on whether the pressure cooker operates at a fixed or variable pressure.

I give below three different methods, depending on the type of pressure cooker.

1. *Visual pressure indicator weight*
The visual pressure indicator weight is a neat device which contains a black plunger which rises and falls as pressure rises and falls. It is marked with three rings and as each ring appears it shows which pressure has been reached. The first ring indicates 5 lb (low) pressure, the second ring, 10 lb

(medium) pressure and the third ring, 15 lb (high) pressure.

After the lid is fitted the weight is placed firmly on the central vent. The heat is then turned on under the pressure cooker. As the liquid boils it creates steam which causes pressure to rise. As soon as the black plunger shows the required ring, the heat is turned down and the plunger will remain steady at that position without any hissing or spluttering. If it does hiss and splutter it means that the heat has not been reduced enough. If you are already using minimum

Fig. 4. One type of visual pressure indicator weight.
Left to right: Off, 5 lb (low,) 10 lb (medium,) 15 lb (high.)

heat, particularly with an electric radiant ring, the pressure cooker should be drawn gently half-way off the ring. If the heat has been turned down too far, pressure will drop and you will see at once when this happens as the black plunger will fall slightly. Increase the heat a little until you have found the correct heat to maintain pressure.

I find that an electric radiant ring tends to retain heat for a short while after it has been turned down, so when I want to cook at 15 lb (high) pressure I reduce the heat as soon as 10 lb (medium) is reached. There is still sufficient heat in the radiant ring to bring the pressure cooker quietly up to the required pressure.

2. *Audible pressure indicator weight*
This type of weight tells you when pressure is reached by the noise it makes. It consists of three parts which are screwed together for cooking at three different pressures. The three pieces together are used for 15 lb (high) pressure. The top piece is removed for 10 lb (medium) pressure and the smallest part is used alone for 5 lb (low) pressure.

After fitting the lid click the weight on to the central vent. Turn on the heat and wait for pressure to rise. As this happens the pressure cooker will start to hiss slightly and as soon as you hear a louder hissing sound this tells you that pressure has been reached and the heat should be reduced

Fig. 5. Audible pressure indicator weight.

until only a gentle mutter is heard. As with the previous type of pressure weight, it may be necessary to draw the pressure cooker slightly off an electric radiant ring to maintain the correct sound. If the pressure cooker becomes silent it means that pressure has dropped and the heat should be increased slightly.

3. *Fixed pressure valve*

This type of valve rotates when pressure is reached and only operates at one pressure (usually $7\frac{1}{2}$ lb). Once the lid is in position place the rotating valve on the air vent. Turn on the heat and, as the liquid boils, so pressure increases. As soon as the rotating valve starts to spin, the heat should be reduced until the valve stops rotating.

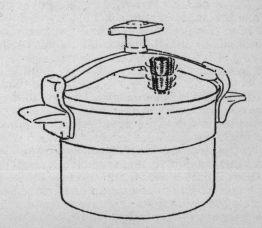

Fig. 6. A spinning valve.
When the valve starts to spin reduce heat until it stops turning.

With all types of pressure cooker the cooking time is calculated from the moment pressure is reached. This can be either from the moment when the black plunger shows the required ring, or when the pressure cooker starts to hiss loudly, or when the rotating valve starts to spin, depending on the type of pressure cooker. How long it takes to reach pressure depends largely on what is inside the pressure cooker. If it only contains a few potatoes and carrots with 300ml ($\frac{1}{2}$ pint) water, it won't take long. If, on the other hand, 1 litre (2 pints) of stock is to be brought to the boil, it will obviously take longer. It is important not to exceed the cooking times, particularly with vegetables, as more delicate food can easily overcook.

At the end of the cooking time the pressure can be reduced in one of two ways.

To reduce pressure quickly the pressure cooker should be stood in a bowl of cold water.

To reduce pressure slowly simply turn off the heat and gently remove the pressure cooker to a cold part of the hob or stand it on a wooden chopping board or heat-resistant surface.

With the visual pressure indicator weight the black plunger will drop down and the automatic air vent in the lid will also fall. This means that the weight can be hooked from the lid, using a fork as it will still be hot.

With the audible pressure indicator weight, wait until it is silent, tip it slightly with a fork and if no steam escapes, lift it off.

With the fixed pressure valve the only way to reduce pressure is to lift the rotating valve slightly to release the steam. The lid should be removed as soon as all the steam has escaped otherwise it remains tightly sealed and can only be removed by bringing the contents of the pressure cooker back to boiling point.

Most recipes give instructions on how to reduce pressure but, as a general guide, the quick method is used for food which will spoil if over-cooked and also for food cooked in a small amount of liquid. The slow method should be used when cooking food such as soups, dried beans and peas, and rice or cereal. All of these are quite liable to froth up a lot during quick pressure reduction and could block safety devices, with unpleasant consequences.

When pressure cooking, remember that for the food to cook there must be room for the steam to circulate. That is why you shouldn't fill a pressure cooker more than two-thirds full of solid food such as vegetables. In the case of recipes containing a lot of liquid such as soups, casseroles, milk puddings, rice and jam, the pressure cooker should not be filled more than half full, otherwise there is a danger that the mixture could froth up and block the vent pipe and safety vent.

HOW TO CARE FOR YOUR PRESSURE COOKER

Each time you use your pressure cooker check that the vent pipe and other safety devices are not blocked and are free to operate.

After using your pressure cooker wash the base in hot, soapy water, rinse and dry. Before washing the lid ensure that the weight has been removed as it would become damaged if it were immersed in water. The rubber-like sealing gasket should be removed and washed too.

As with all aluminium pans the inside will become rather dull and discoloured in time. This is perfectly harmless and due to minerals naturally present in hard water areas. It can easily be removed by adding lemon juice to the water when steaming puddings.

The gasket may shrink slightly after a considerable time and so it is a good idea to stretch it occasionally, before cooking, while it is still cold. If in time steam starts to escape from under the lid it probably means that the gasket needs replacing. This, along with other spare parts, can be obtained direct from the manufacturer if you can't find them at a local shop.

When putting away your pressure cooker ensure that the lid lies upside down on top of the base. This allows air to circulate and prevents a musty smell forming which would be the case if the lid were sealed on. As the weight is precious make sure it is kept somewhere safe where it can't be damaged.

HOW TO ADAPT YOUR RECIPES TO PRESSURE COOKING

The easiest way is to refer to similar recipes in this book or in the manufacturer's instruction book, and follow the same method. If in doubt work out which ingredient needs the longest cooking time and use that as your guide.

If the quantity of food is increased it isn't necessary to extend the cooking time. The time should only be extended if cooking a larger joint of meat or steamed pudding where the heat has to penetrate a greater bulk. It is the length of cooking time which governs how much liquid is needed and manufacturers give instructions in their books.

Remember that when pressure cooking stews and casseroles there won't be as much evaporation as with conventional cooking, so you won't need quite so much liquid. At the same time, don't forget to include at least the minimum amount of liquid recommended by the manufacturer.

If a thicker stew or meat dish is preferred the food may be thickened slightly before cooking using no more than 25g (1 oz) flour, otherwise the steam won't circulate adequately and the food may burn on the bottom. Stir the thickened stew well before pressure cooking to prevent food sticking. If further thickening is required, this should be done after cooking.

Both imperial and metric measurements are given for each recipe. As they are not exact equivalents you should follow one set and not change in mid recipe. Unless stated otherwise spoon measurements are intended as levelled, not heaped.

2

Soup making, like bread making and growing your own vegetables, has become very popular over the last few years. Why do people bother? If you've tasted bread fresh from the oven and beans fresh from the garden you will understand why people take the trouble to make their own soup. But is it trouble? Certainly not if you use a pressure cooker. With conventional soup-making the preparation and finishing off are often the shortest parts of the whole process. It's the long simmering that takes the time and ties you to the kitchen.

With a pressure cooker soups can be ready in minutes. Lettuce soup for example cooks in 7 minutes. It's a delicious soup, eaten hot or chilled, and a boon to gardeners.

Once you have tried home-made soup you won't want to use tins or packets again. Furthermore you will become Scrooge-like about leftovers and vegetable peelings. Well, washed peelings make an ideal base for a soup so don't waste their goodness.

When a recipe calls for stock, don't automatically turn to a stock cube. With your pressure cooker you can prepare real stock in 30 to 40 minutes. Apart from a rather smug feeling of cooking 'properly' there is no doubt that the flavour is much better especially for more delicately flavoured dishes.

When experimenting with your own favourite soup recipes, I suggest you follow these guidelines for best results.

The trivet is not needed when making soup or stock as the idea is to mingle all the flavours together in the liquid.

Don't fill your pressure cooker more than half full of liquid as it needs room to boil up when cooking. When cooking soup for a large number, make sure that the liquid level doesn't exceed the half-way mark and add the rest of the liquid at the end of the cooking time, bringing the soup to the boil again in the open pressure cooker.

When reducing pressure do this slowly at room temperature. Simply switch off the heat and gently move the pressure cooker to a cool ring.

When converting your own recipes, remember there is less evaporation with pressure cooking. This means that you don't have to allow for the extra liquid which normally boils away. Always remember, though, to ensure that you have in your pressure cooker at least the minimum amount of liquid recommended by your manufacturer's instructions – usually 300ml ($\frac{1}{2}$ pint).

Season in moderation before pressure cooking the soup.

It is always easier to add more salt and pepper at the end rather than try to correct an over-salty soup.

Always add the thickening at the end of the cooking.

More flavour is obtained from bones if they are cut small, so ask your butcher to chop them for you.

The following should not be included when making a basic stock: green vegetables, milk, gravy, thickened sauces, bread or potatoes.

When preparing soup in quantity for the freezer please refer to

the earlier point about not filling above the half-way mark.
Instead of adding the extra liquid at the end of the cooking it
is a good idea to freeze the soup in its concentrated form as it
takes up less space. Add the remaining liquid when thawing
and re-heating.

When calculating the cooking time for your own soup recipes,
compare the ingredients with those of the following recipes.
It is the longest cooking ingredient which will dictate the
time at 15 lb (high) pressure.

STOCK

Makes 550ml (1 *pint*)   40 *minutes at* 15 *lb* (*high*)

This stock will be more or less concentrated depending on
the amount of bones used. As with soups generally, it is
easier to dilute after cooking rather than make too weak a
stock to start with.

Bones, cooked or uncooked
or
poultry carcass, cooked or uncooked
550ml (1 pint) water
2 carrots, scrubbed and sliced
1 onion, roughly chopped
6 peppercorns
bouquet garni
1 teaspoon salt

Put the bones into the pressure cooker and add the water.
Bring to the boil in the open pan and remove the scum from
the surface with a spoon. Add the remaining ingredients, fit
the lid and bring to pressure. Cook at 15 lb (high) for 40
minutes. Reduce pressure slowly at room temperature. Cool
slightly, strain into a container and when cold remove the fat
from the top. If you do not intend to use the stock within 3–4
days it is best frozen.

LETTUCE SOUP

Serves 4   7 *minutes at* 15 *lb* (*high*)

Do try this recipe as it is so easy to make and is surprisingly
tasty. Lettuce Soup freezes well and uses up the surplus
lettuces from the garden.

25g (1 oz) butter or margarine
1 onion, finely chopped
1 large potato, diced
1 lettuce, roughly chopped
550ml (1 pint) chicken stock
550ml (1 pint) milk
1 teaspoon salt
pepper

In the pressure cooker gently fry the onion in the fat (butter) until softened but not browned. Add the remaining ingredients and bring to the boil in the open pan. Lower the heat to a simmer, fit the lid and bring to pressure. Cook at 15 lb (high) pressure for 7 minutes. Reduce pressure slowly at room temperature. Cool slightly and liquidize or sieve the soup to a purée. If serving hot, return to a clean pan and reheat, otherwise cool and chill in the refrigerator for serving cold.

WATERCRESS SOUP

Serves 4–6   *7 minutes at* 15 *lb* (*high*)

This is a filling soup and with fresh crusty bread would make a snack meal.

25g (1 oz) butter or margarine
1 onion, finely chopped
450g (1 lb) potatoes, peeled and diced
1 bunch watercress, carefully washed
1 litre (2 pints) water or chicken stock
1 teaspoon salt
cream or top of the milk

In the pressure cooker gently fry in butter the onion and potatoes until softened but not browned. Add the leaves and stalks of the watercress, the water or stock and salt. Fit the lid and bring to pressure. Cook for 7 minutes at 15 lb (high) pressure. Reduce pressure slowly at room temperature. Cool slightly and liquidize or sieve to a purée. Return to the pan to bring to the boil for serving. Just before serving stir in the cream or top of the milk.

CELERY SOUP

Serves 4   10 *minutes at* 15 *lb* (*high*)

For this soup use the whole celery – both stalks and leaves.
25g (1 oz) butter or margarine
1 head of celery, chopped
1 onion, chopped
850ml (1½ pints) water or chicken stock
25g (1 oz) cornflour
300ml (½ pint) milk
1 teaspoon salt
pepper

In the open pressure cooker gently fry the celery and
onion in butter until softened but not browned. Add the
water or chicken stock and seasoning. Fit the lid and bring
to pressure. Cook for 10 minutes at 15 lb (high) pressure.
Reduce pressure slowly at room temperature. Cool and
liquidize or sieve. Blend the cornflour with the milk to make
a smooth mixture and add to the celery. Bring to the boil,
stirring the soup until thickened.

TOMATO SOUP

Serves 4   4 *minutes at* 15 *lb* (*high*)

2 rashers streaky bacon, chopped
1 onion, finely chopped
700g (1½ lb) tomatoes, skinned
550ml (1 pint) water or stock
1 teaspoon sugar
1 teaspoon salt
pepper
Worcestershire sauce
1 tablespoon cornflour
150ml (¼ pint) water (to be kept aside)
chopped parsley

In the open pressure cooker gently fry the bacon until the
fat begins to run. Add the onion and fry until softened but
not browned. Quarter the tomatoes and put them into the
pressure cooker with the water or stock, sugar and seasoning. Add a dash of Worcestershire sauce. Fit the lid and

bring to pressure. Cook for 4 minutes at 15 lb (high) pressure. Reduce pressure slowly at room temperature. Liquidize or sieve the soup. Blend the cornflour with the remaining water to make a thin mixture and add to the tomato soup. Bring to the boil, stirring until thickened. Serve sprinkled with chopped parsley.

VICHYSSOISE

Traditionally this soup is chilled but is equally good served hot.

Serves 4–6   *5 minutes at* 15 *lb* (*high*)

3 large leeks
25g (1 oz) butter or margarine
1 onion, chopped
450g (1 lb) potatoes, diced small
850ml (1½ pints) water or chicken stock
1 teaspoon salt
pepper
300ml (½ pint) single cream
chives to garnish

Carefully wash and chop only the white part of the leeks. Save the green leaves to add to a casserole. In the open pressure cooker gently fry the leeks and onion in the butter, until softened but not browned. Add the potatoes, water or stock, salt and pepper. Fit the lid and bring to pressure. Cook for 5 minutes at 15 lb (high) pressure. Reduce pressure slowly at room temperature. Cool and liquidize or sieve. Chill in the refrigerator and just before serving stir in the cream and chopped chives. If serving hot, do not re-boil the soup after adding the cream.

BROAD BEAN AND BACON

Serves 4   *5 minutes at* 15 *lb* (*high*)

100g (4 oz) streaky bacon, chopped
1 onion, chopped
450g (1 lb) broad beans (weight after shelling)

850ml (1½ pints) water or chicken stock
300ml (½ pint) milk
1 teaspoon salt
pepper
chives to garnish

In the open pressure cooker gently fry the bacon until the fat begins to run. Add the onion and fry gently until softened but not browned. Add the broad beans, water or chicken stock, milk, salt and pepper. Bring to the boil in the open pan then reduce the heat until simmering. Fit the lid and bring to pressure. Cook for 5 minutes at 15 lb (high) pressure. Reduce pressure slowly at room temperature. Cool and liquidize or sieve. Re-heat and serve garnished with chopped chives.

MINESTRONE

Serves 4–6   **8 *minutes* at 15 *lb* (*high*)**

The ingredients for this soup can be varied, depending on what is in season, but as you can see the ideal Minestrone contains a wide variety of vegetables.

2 rashers streaky bacon, chopped
1 tablespoon olive oil
1 onion, finely chopped
1 clove garlic, crushed (optional)
3 carrots, diced
¼ cabbage, finely shredded
4 sticks celery, thinly sliced
25g (1 oz) peas
1 tablespoon tomato purée
1 teaspoon salt
pepper
1 litre (2 pints) water or chicken stock
50g (2 oz) macaroni or broken pieces of spaghetti
grated Parmesan cheese (optional)

In the open pressure cooker gently fry the bacon until the fat begins to run. Add the oil and the vegetables and fry gently until softened but not browned. Add the tomato purée, seasoning, water or chicken stock and the pasta. Fit the lid and bring to pressure. Cook for 8 minutes at 15 lb (high) pressure. Reduce pressure slowly at room temperature. If wished, serve sprinkled with Parmesan cheese.

MIXED VEGETABLE SOUP

Serves 4–6   10 *minutes at* 15 *lb (high)*

This can be a main course soup and vegetables can be varied with the seasons.

25g (1 oz) butter or margarine
2 onions, finely chopped
4 large carrots cut into 10mm ($\frac{1}{2}$ inch) slices
2 large parsnips cut into 10mm ($\frac{1}{2}$ inch) slices
4 large potatoes cut into 10mm ($\frac{1}{2}$ inch) dice
2 leeks, carefully washed and chopped (use green leaves too)
1 litre (2 pints) beef stock
1 teaspoon salt
pepper
Worcestershire sauce, a dash

In the open pressure cooker gently fry the onions in the butter until softened but not browned. Add all the remaining ingredients, fit the lid and bring to pressure. Cook for 10 minutes at 15 lb (high) pressure. Reduce pressure slowly at room temperature and serve.

FRENCH ONION SOUP

Serves 4   4 *minutes at* 15 *lb (high)*

50g (2 oz) butter or margarine
450g (1 lb) onions, thinly sliced
1 litre (2 pints) beef stock
1 teaspoon salt
pepper
4 slices of French bread
grated cheese

In the open pressure cooker gently fry the onions in the butter until golden brown (10 minutes approx.). Add the stock and seasoning, fit the lid and bring to pressure. Cook for 4 minutes at 15 lb (high) pressure. Reduce pressure slowly at room temperature. Sprinkle cheese on the slices of bread and toast under the grill until the cheese begins to brown. Float a slice of bread, cheese side uppermost, on each bowl of soup.

CARROT AND ORANGE SOUP

Serves 4–6   5 *minutes at* 15 *lb* (*high*)

This may sound an odd combination but it is well worth trying for a change.

25g (1 oz) butter or margarine
1 onion, finely chopped
700g (1½ lb) carrots, thinly sliced
850ml (1½ pints) water or chicken stock
grated rind and juice of 2 oranges
1 teaspoon salt
pepper
1 teaspoon sugar
chopped parsley for garnish

In the open pressure cooker gently fry the onion in the butter until softened but not browned. Add the carrots, water or stock, grated orange rind, salt, pepper and sugar. Fit the lid and bring to pressure. Cook for 5 minutes at 15 lb (high) pressure. Reduce pressure slowly at room temperature. Add the orange juice, cool slightly and liquidize or sieve. Re-heat for serving and sprinkle with parsley.

LENTIL SOUP

Serves 4   10 *minutes at* 15 *lb* (*high*)

Remember when pressure cooking dried seeds such as lentils it is not necessary to soak them beforehand.

25g (1 oz) butter or margarine
1 onion, chopped
100g (4 oz) lentils
1 litre (2 pints) chicken stock
2 tablespoons tomato purée
1 teaspoon salt
pepper
bay leaf (optional)

In the open pressure cooker gently fry the onion in the butter until golden brown. Add the remaining ingredients. Fit the lid and bring to pressure. Cook for 10 minutes at 15 lb (high) pressure. Reduce pressure slowly at room temperature, cool slightly and liquidize or sieve. Re-heat before serving.

PEA AND BACON

Serves 4–6 · 15 *minutes at* 15 *lb* (*high*)

With a pressure cooker it is not necessary to soak the peas overnight. Soak them for 1 hour covered with plenty of boiling water.

4 rashers streaky bacon, chopped
1 large onion, chopped
175g (6 oz) dried split peas, soaked and drained
1 litre (2 pints) chicken stock
sprig of mint
1 teaspoon salt
pepper
cream or top of the milk

In the open pressure cooker gently fry the bacon until the fat begins to run. Add the onion and cook gently until golden brown. Add the peas, stock, mint and seasoning. Bring to the boil then lower heat to simmering. Fit the lid and bring to pressure. Cook for 15 minutes at 15 lb (high) pressure. Reduce pressure slowly at room temperature. Remove the mint. Cool slightly and liquidize or sieve. Re-heat and just before serving stir in a little cream or top of the milk.

FISH STOCK

15 *minutes at* 15 *lb* (*high*)

1 fish head and trimmings
1 onion, chopped
1 celery stick, sliced
6 peppercorns

parsley
1 litre (2 pints) water
bouquet garni
1 teaspoon salt

Wash the fish head and trimmings and put into the pressure cooker with the remaining ingredients. Fit the lid and bring to pressure. Cook for 15 minutes at 15 lb (high) pressure. Reduce pressure slowly at room temperature. Strain the stock and use the same day, otherwise freeze in double packaging.

MEDITERRANEAN FISH SOUP

Serves 4   5 *minutes at* 15 *lb (high)*

Try this as a main course soup with hot herb or garlic bread. Make up the fish weight with at least two different types of fish.

700g (1½ lb) fish such as whiting, plaice or cod
1 tablespoon olive oil
1 onion, sliced
1 clove garlic, crushed (optional)
1 carrot, thinly sliced
227g (8 oz) tin of tomatoes
850ml (1½ pints) fish stock
150ml (¼ pint) dry white wine
1 slice of lemon peel
1 teaspoon salt
pepper
chopped parsley for garnish

Wash the fish and remove the skin and bones to make the fish stock (see page 28). Cut the fish into 50mm (2 in) chunks. In the open pressure cooker heat the oil and gently fry the onion until softened but not browned. Add the crushed garlic, if wished, and the carrot. Gently fry for a minute then add the fish, tomatoes with their juice, stock, wine, lemon peel and seasoning. Fit the lid and bring to pressure. Cook for 5 minutes at 15 lb (high) pressure. Reduce pressure slowly at room temperature. Remove lemon peel, adjust seasoning and sprinkle with parsley.

OXTAIL SOUP

Serves 4   40 *minutes at* 15 *lb* (*high*)

25g (1 oz) lard
1 oxtail, jointed by the butcher
2 carrots, sliced
2 celery stalks, sliced
1 large onion, sliced
bouquet garni
1 tablespoon tomato purée
1 litre (2 pints) beef stock
1 teaspoon salt
pepper
1 tablespoon cornflour
1 tablespoon lemon juice

In the open pressure cooker fry the oxtail in the lard until browned on all sides. Add the vegetables and continue to fry until they are golden brown. Add the bouquet garni, purée, stock, salt and pepper. Fit the lid and bring to pressure. Cook for 40 minutes at 15 lb (high) pressure. Reduce pressure slowly at room temperature. Strain the soup and leave to cool. Remove the meat from the bone and chop into small pieces. When the soup has cooled remove the fat from the surface. In a small bowl blend the cornflour with 2 or 3 tablespoons of the cold soup to make a thin paste. Add this to the soup with the chopped meat and lemon juice and bring to the boil stirring continuously until thickened.

SCOTCH BROTH

Serves 4   20 *minutes at* 15 *lb* (*high*)

This would make a main course soup if you were to double the amount of meat. This would still take the same time to cook.

225g (8 oz) middle neck of lamb
1 litre (2 pints) water
50g (2 oz) pearl barley
1 large onion, finely chopped
1 carrot, diced

1 celery stick, thinly sliced
1 turnip, diced
1 teaspoon salt
pepper

Cut from the meat as much fat as possible. Remove from the bones as much meat as you can and chop it up. Put the meat and bones into the open pressure cooker and add the water. Bring to the boil and remove any scum from the surface. Add the remaining ingredients, fit the lid and bring to pressure. Cook for 20 minutes at 15 lb (high) pressure. Reduce pressure slowly at room temperature. Take out the bones and remove any remaining meat. Return this meat to the soup and serve.

MULLIGATAWNY

Serves 4   5 *minutes at* 15 *lb* (*high*)

This soup can be as 'hot' as you like, depending on how much curry powder you use.

25g (1 oz) butter or margarine
1 onion, chopped
1 carrot, diced
3 teaspoons curry powder, for example
1 litre (2 pints) beef stock
1 tablespoon tomato purée
1 tablespoon mango chutney
2 teaspoons cornflour

In the open pressure cooker gently fry the onion and carrot in the butter until softened but not browned. Stir in the curry powder and continue to cook over a gentle heat for 2–3 minutes. Gradually stir in the stock, purée and chutney. Fit the lid and bring to pressure. Cook for 5 minutes at 15 lb (high) pressure. Reduce pressure slowly at room temperature. Cool slightly and liquidize or sieve. Blend the cornflour with a little cold water to make a thin paste. Add to the soup and bring to the boil, stirring continuously until thickened.

COCK-A-LEEKIE

Serves 4   *7 minutes at 15 lb (high)*

2 chicken joints
1 litre (2 pints) water or chicken stock
1 onion, finely chopped
4 leeks, chopped in 25mm (1 inch) slices
4 prunes, stoned
1 teaspoon salt
pepper
1 tablespoon lemon juice

Cut most of the meat off the bones and put both into the pressure cooker with the water. Bring to the boil and remove any scum which floats to the surface. Add the remaining ingredients. Fit the lid and bring to pressure. Cook for 7 minutes at 15 lb (high) pressure. Reduce pressure slowly at room temperature. Take out the meat and bones and remove any remaining chicken on the bone. Chop the meat small and return it to the soup for serving.

CHICKEN SOUP WITH HERB DUMPLINGS

Serves 6   *10 minutes per 450g (1 lb)*
                                          at 15 lb (high)
                                     15 minutes steaming

Soup   *Dumplings*
1 small boiling fowl   75g (3 oz) self-raising flour
1 litre (2 pints) water   25g (1 oz) shredded suet
1 large onion, sliced   pinch of salt
2 carrots, sliced   pepper
2 sticks celery, sliced   1 teaspoon mixed herbs
bay leaf   milk to mix
1 teaspoon salt
pepper

Weigh the chicken and put into the pressure cooker with the water. Bring to the boil. Reduce heat to a simmer and remove any scum from the surface. Add the remaining soup ingredients, fit the lid and bring to pressure. Cook at 15 lb (high) pressure. The cooking time will depend on the size of the bird and should be calculated at 10 minutes per 450g (1 lb).

While the soup is cooking prepare the dumplings. Sieve the flour into a mixing basin, add the suet, seasoning and herbs. Stir well with a fork to mix and slowly add enough milk to make a scone-like dough. Cut the dough into twelve equal portions and with lightly floured hands shape them into little balls.

After cooking the soup reduce pressure slowly at room temperature. Take out the chicken and remove the meat from the bones. Cut into small pieces and return the meat to the pressure cooker.

Bring the soup to the boil in the open pressure cooker and place the dumplings on top. Fit the lid *without the weight*, reduce the heat until only a thin stream of steam escapes and steam for 15 minutes.

CHICKEN AND MUSHROOM SOUP

Serves 4   5 *minutes at* 15 *lb* (*high*)

This soup is best made with real chicken stock as it does not overwhelm the delicate flavour of the mushrooms.

1 litre (2 pints) chicken stock
1 heaped tablespoon long grain rice, washed
1 teaspoon salt
pepper
100g (4 oz) button mushrooms, wiped and sliced
chives, chopped for garnish

Put the stock, rice, seasoning and mushrooms into the pressure cooker. Fit the lid and bring to pressure. Cook for 5 minutes at 15 lb (high) pressure. Reduce pressure slowly at room temperature. Sprinkle with chives to serve.

3

MEAT

A pressure cooker is a tremendous advantage when cooking meat. Not only is the cooking time less than with conventional methods, but the super-heated steam penetrates the meat to make it really tender. Very little steam escapes during pressure cooking, so all the flavour is trapped inside.

Pressure cooking is a moist cooking method, therefore you can't bake or roast as in an oven. You can boil, braise, casserole, stew and pot roast. This chapter includes a variety of meat recipes from Pressed Tongue and Steak and Kidney

Pudding to Blanquette of Veal and Stuffed Breast of Lamb.
There are a number of points you should bear in mind
when adapting your own meat recipes to pressure cooking:

Trivet: This is not used when cooking stews or casseroles.
Pressure: Use 15 lb (high) pressure and generally reduce
pressure quickly after cooking unless the recipe uses a large
quantity of liquid, or recommends otherwise.
Quantity: Ingredients may be increased but ensure they
don't fill more than two thirds of the pressure cooker.
Time: This is influenced very much by the quality of the
meat, its size and thickness. You will soon get a 'feel' for
timing but use these recipes as a guide. There is no need to
increase the cooking time if the ingredients are increased for
stews or casseroles.
Thickening: Meat may be tossed in a tablespoon of seasoned
flour before cooking, to give a slightly thicker gravy, but if
really thick stews are preferred, extra thickening must be
carried out *after* pressure cooking, using blended flour or
cornflour. Too much thickening before cooking would re-
strict the amount of steam to circulate, with the risk that
food could stick to the base.
Liquid: Remember that there is less evaporation compared
with oven or hob cooking. Consequently your adapted
recipes won't need more than the recommended minimum
of liquid. As a general rule this is 300ml ($\frac{1}{2}$ pint) for the first
20 minutes and 150ml ($\frac{1}{4}$ pint) for each extra 15 minutes
cooking.
Pot roasting: When choosing a joint of meat for pot roasting,
ensure that it will fit inside your pressure cooker without
blocking any of the air vents. Joints over 1·5kg (3 lb) are not
really suitable for pressure cooking as the outside will over-
cook before the centre is done. Follow the general method
for Pot Roast, given on page 42, and use the table below as a
guide to times and liquid.

	450g (1 lb)	1kg (2 lb)	1·5kg (3 lb)
Beef, lamb, mutton, pork, veal	300ml ($\frac{1}{2}$ pt) 15 minutes	425ml ($\frac{3}{4}$ pt) 30 minutes	550ml (1 pt) 45 minutes
Bacon, ham	300ml ($\frac{1}{2}$ pt) 12 minutes	300ml ($\frac{1}{2}$ pt) 24 minutes	425ml ($\frac{3}{4}$ pt) 36 minutes

Freezing

The size of the pressure cooker enables you to cook at least 8 portions, depending on its capacity. When cooking in bulk for the freezer, bear in mind the following points:

Garlic reduces the storage time to 1 month, therefore omit for longer storage.

Do not thicken before freezing. It is best done after re-heating, using cornflour.

Freeze in single or double portions.

If food is to be re-heated from frozen in the pressure cooker, it should be frozen in shallow containers of a size that will fit inside the pressure cooker. This helps reduce the re-heating time, which would be much greater were the food frozen in square blocks.

To re-heat, put 150ml ($\frac{1}{4}$ pint) water in the pressure cooker, without the trivet. Remove the portions from their containers and place in the water. Fit the lid and bring to pressure. The re-heating time will depend on the size of the portion, but as a general rule, cook for 20 minutes at 15 lb (high) pressure. Reduce pressure slowly at room temperature. Thicken before serving. If aluminium foil containers are used to contain the frozen food, these may be stood on the trivet over 300ml ($\frac{1}{2}$ pint) water and pressure cooked for 20 minutes at 15 lb (high) pressure.

BEEF AND VEGETABLE STEW

Serves 4   15 *minutes at* 15 *lb* (*high*)

25g (1 oz) lard
2 onions, chopped
700g (1$\frac{1}{2}$ lb) stewing steak, cubed
25g (1 oz) flour
225g (8 oz) carrots, sliced
450g (1 lb) potatoes, thickly sliced
1 turnip, sliced
2 parsnips, sliced
2 leeks, (including green leaves), sliced
550ml (1 pint) stock
1 teaspoon salt
pepper
bay leaf
1 tablespoon parsley, chopped for garnish

Fry the onions in the lard in the open pressure cooker, without the trivet, until softened but not browned. Toss the meat in the flour and brown on all sides in the pressure cooker. Add all the remaining ingredients except for the parsley. Fit the lid and bring to pressure. Cook for 15 minutes at 15 lb (high) pressure. Reduce pressure quickly in cold water. Remove bay leaf and serve garnished with parsley.

OXTAIL CASSEROLE

Serves 3   40 *minutes at* 15 *lb* (*high*)

This can be a rather fatty dish and would therefore be better cooked a day in advance so that the cold fat could be skimmed off before re-heating.

25g (1 oz) lard
1 onion, chopped
1 oxtail, jointed by the butcher
25g (1 oz) flour
225g (8 oz) carrots, sliced
550ml (1 pint) stock
bouquet garni
2 tablespoons tomato purée
1 teaspoon salt
pepper
1 teaspoon lemon juice

In the open pressure cooker, without the trivet, fry the onion in the lard until golden brown. Remove the onion from the pressure cooker using a slotted spoon. Trim as much fat from the oxtail as possible. Toss it in the flour and brown on all sides in the pressure cooker. Remove from the pressure cooker using a slotted spoon. Pour away any remaining fat. Return the onion and oxtail to the pressure cooker and add the carrots, stock, bouquet garni, tomato purée, salt and pepper. Fit the lid and bring to pressure. Cook for 40 minutes at 15 lb (high) pressure. Reduce pressure quickly in cold water. Remove the bouquet garni and add the lemon juice.

GOULASH

Serves 4   *15 minutes at* 15 *lb* (*high*)

25g (1 oz) cooking oil
2 onions, chopped
700g (1½ lb) stewing steak, cubed
25g (1 oz) flour
3 tablespoons paprika pepper
300ml (½ pint) stock
2 tablespoons tomato purée
1 tablespoon dried mixed herbs
bay leaf
1 teaspoon salt

In the open pressure cooker, without the trivet, gently fry the onions in the oil until golden brown. Toss the meat in the flour and brown on all sides in the pressure cooker. Add the paprika pepper and cook on a low heat stirring for 1 minute. Add the stock, purée, mixed herbs, bay leaf and salt. Fit the lid and bring to pressure. Cook for 15 minutes at 15 lb (high) pressure. Reduce pressure quickly in cold water. Remove the bay leaf.

BEEF CURRY

Serves 4   *15 minutes at* 15 *lb* (*high*)

25g (1 oz) lard
1 onion, finely chopped
1 clove garlic, crushed (optional)
1 stick celery, sliced
700g (1½ lb) stewing steak, cubed
25g (1 oz) flour
1 tablespoon curry powder
300ml (½ pint) stock
1 apple, peeled, cored and chopped
1 tablespoon tomato ketchup
1 teaspoon lemon juice
1 heaped tablespoon chutney
25g (1 oz) sultanas

In the open pressure cooker, without the trivet, gently fry the onion until softened but not browned. Add the garlic (if used) and celery and fry gently for a minute. Toss the meat in the flour and brown on all sides in the pressure cooker. Add the curry powder and cook on a low heat, stirring, until the fat has been absorbed. Add the remaining ingredients. Fit the lid and bring to pressure. Cook for 15 minutes at 15 lb (high) pressure. Reduce pressure quickly in cold water.

BEEF IN BEER

Serves 4   15 *minutes at* 15 *lb* (*high*)

25g (1 oz) butter or margarine
2 rashers streaky bacon, chopped
2 onions, chopped
700g (1½ lb) stewing steak, cubed
25g (1 oz) flour
300ml (½ pint) brown ale
150ml (¼ pint) stock
1 teaspoon French mustard
2 teaspoons sugar
1 teaspoon salt
pepper
bouquet garni

In the open pressure cooker, without the trivet, gently fry the bacon and onions in the butter until softened but not browned. Toss the meat in the flour and brown on all sides in the pressure cooker. Add the beer, stock, mustard, sugar, seasoning and bouquet garni. Fit the lid and bring to pressure. Cook for 15 minutes at 15 lb (high) pressure. Reduce pressure quickly in cold water. Remove the bouquet garni.

BOLOGNESE SAUCE

Serves 4   10 *minutes at* 15 *lb* (*high*)

This is a favourite of mine for bulk cooking as it can be used as a basis for so many other dishes, such as Spaghetti Bolognese, Lasagne, Stuffed Peppers or Cottage Pie. If freezing for long, omit the garlic.

25g (1 oz) butter or margarine
2 rashers streaky bacon, chopped
1 onion, chopped
1 clove garlic, crushed (optional)
2 stalks celery, thinly sliced
700g (1½ lb) lean minced beef
397g (14 oz) can tomatoes
150ml (¼ pint) beef stock
1 teaspoon Worcestershire sauce
1 teaspoon salt
pepper
1 teaspoon oregano
bay leaf

In the open pressure cooker, without the trivet, gently fry the bacon, onion, garlic and celery in the butter until softened but not browned. Remove from the pressure cooker using a slotted spoon. Drain away remaining fat. Add the meat and brown on all sides. Return the fried vegetables to the pressure cooker and add all the remaining ingredients. Fit the lid and bring to pressure. Cook for 10 minutes at 15 lb (high) pressure. Reduce pressure quickly in cold water. Remove the bay leaf.

STEAK AND KIDNEY PUDDING

Serves 4–6　　　　　　*Filling: 15 minutes at 15 lb (high)*
　　　　　　　　　　　　Pudding: 20 minutes steaming
　　　　　　　　　　　　　30 minutes at 5 lb (low)

Filling
25g (1 oz) lard
1 onion, chopped
700g (1½ lb) stewing steak, cubed
25g (1 oz) flour
100g (4 oz) ox kidney, sliced
225g (8 oz) mushrooms
1 teaspoon salt
pepper
300ml (½ pint) stock or Guinness

Suet pastry
200g (8 oz) self-raising flour
½ teaspoon salt
100g (4 oz) shredded suet
150ml (¼ pint) water

In the open pressure cooker, without the trivet, gently fry the onion in the lard until softened but not browned. Toss the meat in the flour and brown on all sides in the pressure cooker. Add the mushrooms, seasoning and stock or Guinness. Fit the lid and bring to pressure. Cook for 15 minutes at 15 lb (high) pressure. Reduce pressure quickly in cold water. Turn into a container and allow to cool while preparing the suet pastry.

Mix together the flour, salt and suet. Stir in the water, gradually, using sufficient to make a scone-like dough. Reserve one third of the dough for the lid and roll the remaining dough into a circle large enough to line a 1 litre (2 pint) pudding basin. Grease the basin and line it with the pastry. Using a slotted spoon fill the basin to within 25mm (1 in) of the top with the meat mixture, adding 3 tablespoons of the gravy. Reserve the remainder for serving separately. Roll out the small piece of pastry to make a lid. Moisten the edges of the pastry and firmly crimp the lid into position, ensuring that there is a space up to the rim of the basin to allow the pastry to rise. Cover securely with a double layer of greased greaseproof paper or a single layer of aluminium foil. Put the trivet and 1 litre (2 pints) water into the cleaned pressure cooker. Stand the basin on the trivet. Fit the lid *without* the weight in position and steam for 20 minutes on a gentle heat. Fit the weight and bring to pressure. Cook for 30 minutes at 5 lb (low) pressure. Reduce pressure slowly at room temperature. Remove the pudding from the pressure cooker and serve with the heated gravy.

Freezer note: Freeze when cooked. To defrost and re-heat cook for 40 minutes at 5 lb (low) using 1 litre (2 pints) water.

GORTHWISTY STEW

Serves 4   20 *minutes at* 15 *lb* (*high*)
25g (1 oz) butter beans
25g (1 oz) whole dried peas

Gorthwisty Stew contd.
25g (1 oz) lard
2 onions, chopped
700g (1½ lb) stewing steak, cubed
1 parsnip, sliced
2 carrots, sliced
2 potatoes, sliced
50g (2 oz) lentils
25g (1 oz) pearl barley
550ml (1 pint) stock
1 tablespoon tomato purée
1 teaspoon mixed herbs
1 teaspoon salt
pepper

Soak the butter beans and dried peas for 1 hour in a basin, covered with 550ml (1 pint) boiling water. In the open pressure cooker, without the trivet, gently fry the onions until softened but not browned. Add the meat and brown on all sides. Add the remaining ingredients, fit the lid and bring to pressure. Cook for 20 minutes at 15 lb (high) pressure. Reduce pressure quickly in cold water.

POT ROAST

Serves 4–6   30 *minutes at* 15 *lb* (*high*)

1kg (2 lb) rolled top ribs, brisket or shoulder of beef
25g (1 oz) lard
1 onion, sliced
450g (1 lb) potatoes
8 carrots
4 parsnips
1 turnip, cubed
550ml (1 pint) stock
1 teaspoon salt
pepper
1 tablespoon Worcestershire sauce
2 tablespoons tomato purée

Trim the meat of excess fat and in the open pressure cooker, without the trivet, brown the meat on all sides in the lard, turning it frequently to ensure an even colour. Remove from the pressure cooker. Gently fry the onion until softened but not browned. Add the remaining ingredients and stand the meat on this bed of vegetables. Fit the lid and bring to pressure. Cook for 30 minutes at 15 lb (high) pressure. Reduce pressure quickly in cold water. Remove the brisket and place on a serving dish. Remove the vegetables, using a slotted spoon, and place around the meat. Serve the gravy separately.

ITALIAN BRISKET

Serves 4–6   30 *minutes at* 15 *lb* (*high*)

1 rasher streaky bacon
1 teaspoon salt
½ teaspoon black pepper
½ teaspoon rosemary, finely chopped
1 clove garlic, crushed
1kg (2 lb) brisket
25g (1 oz) butter or margarine
1 onion sliced, 2 sticks celery, sliced
425g (15 oz) can tomatoes
2 tablespoons tomato purée
1 tablespoon dried mixed peppers
1 teaspoon salt
black pepper
1 tablespoon cornflour
2 tablespoons water

Cut the bacon cross-ways into matchstick sized pieces. Mix together the salt, pepper, rosemary and garlic. Roll the bacon pieces in this mixture. Trim excess fat from the meat. Using a small, sharp pointed knife, cut in the brisket as many slits as you have pieces of bacon. Stuff the bacon into these slits. In the open pressure cooker, without the trivet, brown the meat on all sides in the fat, turning frequently to ensure an even colour. Remove from the pressure cooker. In the remaining fat fry the onion and celery until softened but not browned. Return the brisket to the pressure cooker and add the can of tomatoes, including the juice, the dried peppers, purée and seasoning. Fit the lid and bring to pressure. Cook for 30 minutes at 15 lb (high) pressure. Reduce pressure quickly in cold water. Remove the brisket to a serving dish. Mix the cornflour with water to make a smooth paste. Add to the sauce and bring to the boil, stirring continuously until thickened. Serve with the sliced brisket.

BARBECUED SPARE RIBS

Serves 4   15 *minutes at* 15 *lb* (*high*)

1 tablespoon oil
1–1·5kg (2–3 lb) pork spare ribs

Sauce
1 onion, finely chopped
1 green pepper, finely chopped
425g (15 oz) can tomatoes
2 tablespoons vinegar
1 tablespoon Worcestershire sauce
1 teaspoon dried mustard
½ teaspoon salt
few drops Tabasco sauce

Using a liquidizer blend together the sauce ingredients.
Cut the spare ribs into single bone pieces with a strip of meat
either side. In the open pressure cooker, without the trivet,
gently fry the pork ribs in the oil until browned on both
sides. Remove the spare ribs and drain away the oil. Return
the spare ribs to the pressure cooker and pour over the
sauce. Fit the lid and bring to pressure. Cook for 15 minutes
at 15 lb (high) pressure. Reduce pressure quickly.

SWEET AND SOUR PORK

Serves 4   15 *minutes at* 15 *lb* (*high*)

25g (1 oz) lard
700g (1½ lb) lean pork, cubed
340g (12 oz) can pineapple chunks
water
4 tablespoons vinegar
75g (3 oz) brown sugar
1 tablespoon soy sauce
½ teaspoon salt
1 green pepper, de-seeded and finely sliced
1 onion, finely sliced
2 tablespoons cornflour
3 tablespoons water

In the open pressure cooker, without the trivet, fry the pork in the lard until browned on all sides. Drain the pineapple, reserving the syrup. Add sufficient water to the syrup to make 300ml (½ pint) liquid and pour into the pressure cooker. Add the vinegar, sugar, soy sauce, salt, onion and green pepper. Bring to the boil, stirring to dissolve the sugar. Fit the lid and bring to pressure. Cook for 15 minutes at 15 lb (high) pressure. Reduce pressure quickly in cold water. Mix the cornflour and water to make a smooth paste. Add the pineapple chunks to the pork and pour over the blended cornflour. Bring to the boil, stirring continuously until thickened.

PORK AND LEMON

Serves 4   15 *minutes at* 15 *lb* (*high*)

25g (1 oz) butter or margarine
1 onion, finely chopped
700g (1½ lb) pie pork, cubed
300ml (½ pint) dry white wine
grated rind of 1 lemon
juice of ½ lemon
¼ teaspoon dried tarragon
1 teaspoon salt
pepper

In the open pressure cooker, without the trivet, gently fry the onion in the butter until softened but not browned. Add the pork and brown on all sides. Add all remaining ingredients. Fit the lid and bring to pressure. Cook for 15 minutes at 15 lb (high) pressure. Reduce pressure quickly in cold water.

BACON AND BEANS

Serves 4   25 *minutes at* 15 *lb* (*high*)

225g (8 oz) dried haricot beans
25g (1 oz) butter or margarine
1 onion, chopped

Bacon and Beans contd.
1 clove garlic, crushed (optional)
1 red pepper, de-seeded and chopped
700g (1½ lb) bacon joint, cubed
397g (14 oz) can tomatoes
150ml (¼ pint) bacon or chicken stock
1 teaspoon brown sugar
1 tablespoon Worcestershire sauce
1 teaspoon dried mustard
1 bay leaf
½ teaspoon salt
pepper

   Place the haricot beans in a deep bowl and cover with
550ml (1 pint) boiling water. Leave to soak for 1 hour. In
the open pressure cooker, without the trivet, gently fry the
onion in the butter until softened but not browned. Add the
garlic, if wished, and the red pepper and fry gently for a
minute. Add the remaining ingredients together with the
drained beans. Fit the lid and bring to pressure. Cook for
25 minutes at 15 lb (high) pressure. Reduce pressure quickly
in cold water.

BOILED BACON OR HAM

12 minutes per 450g (1 lb)
at 15 lb (high)

1 piece of ham or bacon
2 carrots
2 sticks celery, broken in half
1 bay leaf
water (see table page 35)
50g (2 oz) toasted breadcrumbs

   Weigh the meat and calculate the cooking time (see table
page 35). Put in the open pressure cooker without the trivet.
Cover with cold water and bring to the boil. Discard the
water and rinse away the scum. Return the meat to the pressure cooker and add the cooking water, vegetables and bay
leaf. Fit the lid and bring to pressure. Cook for 12 minutes
per 450g (1 lb) at 15 lb (high) pressure. Reduce pressure
slowly at room temperature. Remove the meat from the
pressure cooker, reserving the cooking liquid for use as

stock later. Allow to cool and remove skin. Coat with toasted breadcrumbs.

CIDER BACON

Serves 4–6   30 *minutes at* 15 *lb* (*high*)

1kg (2 lb) bacon joint
425ml (¾ pint) cider
1 onion, sliced
2 sticks celery, sliced
6 black peppercorns
pinch of sage
2 tablespoons cornflour
3 tablespoons water

Trim from the joint as much fat as possible. Place the meat in the open pressure cooker without the trivet. Cover with cold water and bring to the boil. Remove the bacon, discard the water and rinse out the pressure cooker. Return the bacon to the pressure cooker and add the cider, onion, celery, peppercorns and sage. Fit the lid and bring to pressure. Cook for 30 minutes at 15 lb (high) pressure. Reduce pressure quickly in cold water. Remove the bacon to a serving dish. Remove the peppercorns. Mix the cornflour with the water to make a smooth paste. Add to the sauce and bring to the boil, stirring continuously until thickened. Spoon some of the sauce over the bacon and serve the remainder separately.

DEVON LAMB AND POTATO PIE

Serves 4   13 *minutes at* 15 *lb* (*high*)

4 large lamb chops
25g (1 oz) butter or margarine
1 onion, finely chopped
1kg (2 lb) potatoes, sliced
1 teaspoon salt
pepper
2 cooking apples, peeled and sliced
2 teaspoons brown sugar
300ml (½ pint) dry cider

Trim from the chops as much fat as possible. In the open pressure cooker, without the trivet, brown the chops in the butter, on both sides. Remove the chops from the pressure cooker and reserve on one side. Place the onion in a layer on the base of the pressure cooker. Cover with a layer of half the potato and season. Cover with a layer of apple, sprinkle with sugar and top with the final layer of potato. Add the chops, season and pour over the cider. Fit the lid and bring to pressure. Cook for 13 minutes at 15 lb (high) pressure. Reduce pressure quickly in cold water.

LANCASHIRE HOTPOT

Serves 4   15 *minutes at* 15 *lb* (*high*)

1kg (2 lb) potatoes, sliced
1 large onion, sliced
225g (8 oz) carrots, sliced
2 sticks celery, sliced
700g (1½ lb) scrag end or neck of lamb
1 teaspoon salt
pepper
300ml (½ pint) stock

Arrange half the potatoes on the base of the pressure cooker, without the trivet. Season and cover with a layer of onion, carrots and celery. Trim excess fat from the lamb. Arrange over the vegetables and cover with a layer of the remaining potatoes. Season and pour over the stock. Fit the lid and bring to pressure. Cook for 15 minutes at 15 lb (high) pressure. Reduce pressure quickly in cold water.

STUFFED BREAST OF LAMB

This is a cheap cut and it is worth spending a little time with a sharp knife to remove as much fat from the meat as possible.

Serves 4   30 *minutes at* 15 *lb* (*high*)

Stuffing:
25g (1 oz) butter or margarine
1 onion, finely chopped
1 stick celery, finely chopped
100g (4 oz) fresh breadcrumbs
grated rind of 1 lemon
pinch of rosemary
2 tablespoons chopped parsley
½ teaspoon salt
pepper
1 egg, beaten

2 small breasts of lamb, boned by the butcher
   (use the bones for stock)
25g (1 oz) butter or margarine
50g (2 oz) lentils
2 carrots, sliced
1 teaspoon salt
pepper
550ml (1 pint) stock

In a small pan gently fry the onion and celery in the butter until softened but not browned. Mix together all remaining stuffing ingredients and add the onion and celery. Trim surplus fat from the meat. Spread the stuffing evenly over the meat and roll from the narrow end. Secure with string. In the open pressure cooker, without the trivet, brown the rolls in the butter on all sides, turning frequently to ensure an even, golden colour. Add the lentils, carrots, seasoning and stock. Fit the lid and bring to pressure. Cook for 30 minutes at 15 lb (high) pressure. Reduce pressure quickly in cold water. Remove the meat from the pressure cooker and cut each roll in half. Remove the string and pour over the sauce.

SUNSHINE LAMB

Serves 4   15 *minutes at* 15 *lb* (*high*)

25g (1 oz) butter or margarine
1 onion, chopped
700g (1½ lb) boned leg of lamb, cubed
1 tablespoon flour

Sunshine Lamb contd.
300ml (½ pint) stock
2 tablespoons tomato purée
100g (4 oz) dried apricots
1 teaspoon sugar
1 teaspoon salt
pepper

In the open pressure cooker, without the trivet, gently fry the onion in the butter until softened but not browned. Toss the meat in the flour and brown on all sides. Stir in the stock, purée, apricots, sugar and seasoning. Fit the lid and bring to pressure. Cook for 15 minutes at 15 lb (high) pressure. Reduce pressure quickly in cold water.

PRESSED TONGUE

15 minutes per 450g (1 lb)
at 15 lb (high)

1 ox tongue
1 onion
2 carrots
2 sticks celery, snapped in half
1 bay leaf
water

Weigh the tongue and calculate the cooking time. If the tongue has been salted soak in cold water overnight. Put the tongue in the open pressure cooker, without the trivet, and cover with cold water. Bring to the boil and discard the water, rinsing away any scum. Return the tongue to the pressure cooker. Add the vegetables and bay leaf and fill the pressure cooker half full of cold water. Fit the lid and bring to pressure. Cook for 15 minutes per 450g (1 lb) at 15 lb (high) pressure. Reduce pressure slowly at room temperature. Remove the tongue from the pressure cooker and plunge into a bowl of cold water. Remove the skin, gristle and bones. Curl the tongue tightly into a 16-cm (6-in) cake tin or similarly sized dish. Cover with a plate and press with a heavy weight for 24 hours. Turn out of the tin for slicing.

LIVER AND ONIONS

Serves 4   5 *minutes at* 15 *lb* (*high*)

25g (1 oz) lard
4 rashers streaky bacon
3 onions, sliced
700g (1½ lb) lambs liver, sliced
25g (1 oz) flour
300ml (½ pint) stock
1 teaspoon salt
pepper

In the open pressure cooker, without the trivet, fry the
bacon in the lard until crisp. Remove from the pressure
cooker and keep warm. Fry the onions until golden brown.
Toss the liver in the flour and brown on all sides in the pressure cooker. Add the stock and seasoning. Fit the lid and
bring to pressure. Cook for 5 minutes at 15 lb (high) pressure.
Reduce pressure quickly in cold water. Garnish with bacon

LIVER AND ORANGE

The slight tartness of the orange blends well with the rich
flavour of liver.

Serves 4   4 *minutes at* 15 *lb* (*high*)

2 oranges
50g (2 oz) butter or margarine
1 teaspoon sugar
1 onion, chopped
1 clove garlic, crushed (optional)
700g (1½ lb) lambs liver, thinly sliced
25g (1 oz) flour
½ tablespoon thyme
1 tablespoon parsley, chopped
300ml (½ pint) stock
1 teaspoon salt
pepper

Grate the rind of one orange and squeeze its juice. Peel
the second orange and cut the flesh into thin slices. In the
open pressure cooker, using half the fat, gently fry the

orange slices on both sides until softened. Sprinkle with sugar and fry for another minute. Remove from the pressure cooker and keep warm for later. Add the remaining fat and gently fry the onion and garlic (if used) until softened but not browned. Toss the liver in the flour and brown on all sides in the pressure cooker. Sprinkle with the parsley and thyme and add the stock, grated rind, salt and pepper. Fit the lid and bring to pressure. Cook for 4 minutes at 15 lb (high) pressure. Reduce pressure quickly in cold water. Stir in the orange juice and serve garnished with the orange slices.

SAVOURY KIDNEYS

Serves 4   *5 minutes at* 15 lb (*high*)

25g (1 oz) butter or margarine
1 onion, chopped
8 lambs kidneys, halved and cored
25g (1 oz) flour
8 chipolata sausages
300ml ($\frac{1}{2}$ pint) stock
150ml ($\frac{1}{4}$ pint) red wine
1 tablespoon tomato purée
1 bay leaf
1 teaspoon salt
pepper

In the open pressure cooker, without the trivet, gently fry the onion in the butter until softened but not browned. Add the chipolatas and brown on all sides. Toss the kidneys in the flour and brown on both sides in the pressure cooker. Add the stock, wine, purée, bay leaf and seasoning. Fit the lid and bring to pressure. Cook for 5 minutes at 15 lb (high) pressure. Reduce pressure quickly in cold water. Remove the bay leaf and serve.

KIDNEYS WITH MUSHROOMS

Serves 4   *5 minutes at* 15 lb (*high*)

25g (1 oz) butter or margarine
1 onion, chopped
12 lamb kidneys, halved and cored

25g (1 oz) flour
100g (4 oz) button mushrooms
1 tablespoon tomato purée
2 tablespoons sherry
300ml ($\frac{1}{2}$ pint) chicken stock
1 teaspoon salt
pepper

In the open pressure cooker, without the trivet, gently fry the onion until softened but not browned. Toss the kidneys in the flour and brown on both sides. Add the remaining ingredients. Fit the lid and bring to pressure. Cook for 5 minutes at 15 lb (high) pressure. Reduce pressure quickly in cold water.

COUNTRY LIVER PÂTÉ

Serves 4–6   30 *minutes at* 15 *lb* (*high*)

6 slices streaky bacon
225g (8 oz) pigs liver, sliced
100g (4 oz) pork sausagemeat
1 onion, finely chopped
1 clove garlic, crushed (optional)
75g (3 oz) breadcrumbs
$\frac{1}{2}$ teaspoon salt
pepper
$\frac{1}{2}$ teaspoon dried sage
1 egg, beaten
1 tablespoon sherry or brandy

Remove the rinds and, using the back of a knife, stretch the bacon. Line a small loaf tin with the bacon crossways so that at this stage the ends fall loosely over the sides. Blend all the remaining ingredients together using a liquidizer. Alternatively mince the liver finely and mix thoroughly with remaining ingredients. Pour the mixture into the loaf tin and wrap the ends of the bacon over the pâté. Cover securely with aluminium foil. Put 550ml (1 pint) water into the pressure cooker and add the trivet. Stand the loaf tin on the trivet, fit the lid and bring to pressure. Cook for 30 minutes at 15 lb (high) pressure. Reduce pressure slowly at room temperature. Remove the tin from the pressure cooker, loosen the foil and press with a heavy weight until cold. Remove from the tin and serve.

BLANQUETTE OF VEAL

Serves 4   15 *minutes at* 15 *lb* (*high*)

25g (1 oz) butter or margarine
700g (1½ lb) pie veal, cubed
1 carrot sliced
1 stick of celery, sliced
300ml (½ pint) stock
100g (4 oz) button mushrooms
bouquet garni
1 teaspoon salt
pepper
12 button onions
1 tablespoon cornflour
2 tablespoons water
1 egg yolk
2 tablespoons double cream
1 tablespoon lemon juice
1 tablespoon parsley, chopped

In the open pressure cooker, without the trivet, brown the veal in the butter on all sides. Add the carrot, celery, stock, mushrooms, bouquet garni and seasoning. Fit the lid and bring to pressure. Cook for 10 minutes at 15 lb (high) pressure. Reduce pressure quickly in cold water. Add the onions and bring back to pressure for a further 5 minutes. Remove the bouquet garni. Mix the cornflour with the water to make a smooth paste. Add to the veal and bring to the boil, stirring continuously, until thickened. Beat the egg yolk with the cream and lemon juice. Beat in a few tablespoons of hot sauce and mix well. Pour this mixture into the pressure cooker and stir over the lowest heat until the sauce thickens. Do not allow the sauce to boil or it may curdle. Garnish with parsley.

Freezing: Freeze before thickening with the egg yolk, cream and lemon juice. Do this when re-heating.

4

POULTRY AND GAME

The tenderizing effect of pressure cooking is invaluable when cooking poultry and game. A rabbit or pheasant of dubious age, 'bagged' during a day's shooting, can be a mixed blessing if it turns out to be as tough as old boots! This chapter includes a variety of recipes for the more common types of poultry and game, and a table giving typical cooking times to help you adapt your own favourites.

Chicken is reasonably priced and extremely versatile. It can be pressure cooked whole or in joints, in a variety of sauces, in a remarkably short time.

Adapting recipes

Trivet: The trivet is not used when cooking casseroles, but may be used when pot roasting.

Pressure: Use 15 lb (high) pressure and generally reduce pressure quickly after cooking, unless the recipe includes a large quantity of liquid.

Quantity, Thickening and Liquid: See page 35 in the Meat chapter.

Time: Follow the times given in the table. Chicken portions vary in size, therefore I recommend a cooking time of 7–10 minutes, depending on the thickness of the joints. Poultry and game may be stuffed, but remember to weigh the bird after stuffing when calculating the cooking time.

Pot roasting: Follow the general method for Chicken Pot Roast on page 58, varying the time according to the table.

Freezing: All frozen poultry and game must be completely thawed before cooking, otherwise the heat will not penetrate sufficiently to kill bacteria which may be present. When re-heating cooked recipes from frozen, food must be piping hot before serving. Follow the same advice and method for re-heating as given in the Meat chapter, page 36.

Table of cooking times

Chicken, poussin	4–7 minutes
roasting, whole	7 minutes/450g (1 lb)
roasting, jointed	7–10 minutes
boiling, whole	10 minutes/450g (1 lb)
boiling, jointed	15–20 minutes
Duckling, whole	12–15 minutes/450g (1 lb)
jointed	10–12 minutes
Grouse, young	10 minutes
Grouse, old	15 minutes
Hare, jointed	35–40 minutes
Minimum 550ml/1 pt. liquid required	
Rabbit, jointed	20–25 minutes
Partridge, Pheasant, whole	7–10 minutes
jointed	5–7 minutes
Pigeons, halved	20–25 minutes
Venison	20–25 minutes/450g (1 lb)

CHICKEN LIVER PÂTÉ

Serves 6–8   30 *minutes at* 15 *lb* (*high*)

This makes a delicious 'starter' for a dinner party. It can be made weeks in advance and frozen. Storage time is 6 weeks. Allow to thaw at room temperature for 2–3 hours.

2 bay leaves
8 rashers streaky bacon, de-rinded thin-cut
350g (12 oz) chicken livers
1 clove garlic, crushed (optional)
1 egg, beaten
2 tablespoons cream or top of the milk
½ teaspoon mixed herbs
1 teaspoon salt
black pepper
1 tablespoon sherry

Grease a 450g (1-lb) loaf tin. Lay the 2 bay leaves on the base of the tin. Line the tin with the rashers of bacon lying cross-ways. In a liquidizer blend together all the remaining ingredients. Alternatively, mince the liver before mixing with the remaining ingredients. Pour into the loaf tin and cover securely with greased aluminium foil. Put 550ml (1 pint) water into the pressure cooker, with the trivet. Stand the loaf tin on the trivet, fit the lid and bring to pressure. Cook for 30 minutes at 15 lb (high) pressure. Reduce pressure slowly at room temperature. Allow the pâté to cool under a weight. Turn out when cold.

CHICKEN or TURKEY CURRY

Use the ingredients and method for Beef Curry (page 38) but substitute cooked chicken or turkey for the beef. Add a small can of pineapple chunks, using the juice as part of the liquid required in the recipe.

CHICKEN POT ROAST

Serves 4–6   *7 minutes per* 450g *(*1 *lb)*
                                    at 15 *lb* (*high*)

1½kg (3 lb) roasting chicken
25g (1 oz) butter or margarine
300ml (½ pint) water or chicken stock
1 small onion, chopped
1 carrot, chopped
bay leaf
1 teaspoon salt
pepper

If using a frozen chicken, ensure that it is thoroughly
thawed and that the giblets have been removed. Rinse and
pat dry. Ensure that the bird is firmly trussed. Melt the
butter in the open pressure cooker, without the trivet, and
brown the chicken on all sides, turning it to ensure an even
colour. Remove from the pressure cooker and drain away
the remaining butter. Pour the water into the pressure
cooker and add the trivet and chicken. Sprinkle with the
remaining ingredients, fit the lid and bring to pressure. Cook
for 7 minutes per 450g (1 lb) at 15 lb (high) pressure. Reduce
pressure quickly in cold water. Remove the flavouring ingredients. Remove the chicken and keep warm. Use the
strained stock to make the gravy.

Whole potatoes and carrots may be cooked with the
chicken by reducing pressure 7 minutes before the end of the
cooking time, adding the vegetables and bringing back to
pressure for a further 7 minutes' cooking.

CHICKEN TARRAGON

Follow the same basic method as for Chicken Pot Roast
(above). Sprinkle over the chicken a teaspoon of dried
tarragon and the grated rind of one lemon. Add the juice of
half a lemon to the stock. After cooking, strain the sauce and
thicken if wished.

SUMMERTIME CHICKEN

Serves 4   7–10 *minutes at* 15 *lb* (*high*)

25g (1 oz) butter or margarine
1 onion, sliced
4 chicken portions
225g (8 oz) tomatoes, skinned and quartered
1 green pepper, de-seeded and cut into strips
450g (1 lb) courgettes, thickly sliced
150ml ($\frac{1}{4}$ pint) chicken stock
1 tablespoon tomato purée
1 teaspoon salt
pepper
1 teaspoon oregano

In the open pressure cooker, without the trivet, gently fry the onion in the butter until softened but not browned. Add the chicken and brown on all sides. Add all remaining ingredients, fit the lid and bring to pressure. Cook for 7–10 minutes at 15 lb (high) pressure. Reduce pressure quickly in cold water.

CHICKEN RISOTTO

Serves 4   8 *minutes at* 15 *lb* (*high*)

If you are using the left-overs from Sunday's roast chicken, strip the carcass of the meat for the risotto and use the bones to make the stock.

50g (2 oz) butter or margarine
1 onion, chopped
1 stick celery, thinly sliced
175g (6 oz) long grain rice
550ml (1 pint) chicken stock
1 tablespoon dried mixed herbs
350g (12 oz) cooked chicken , cubed
1 teaspoon salt
pepper
100g (4 oz) frozen peas

In the open pressure cooker, without the trivet, gently fry the onion and celery in the butter until softened but not browned. Add the rice and stir fry for 2–3 minutes. Add the remaining ingredients, except for the peas, and bring to the boil, stirring continuously. Reduce the heat to a medium setting, fit the lid and bring to pressure on that heat. Cook for 8 minutes at 15 lb (high) pressure. Reduce pressure slowly at room temperature. Remove the lid and add the frozen peas. Cook on a medium heat for 5 minutes, stirring continuously and fluffing up the rice.

COQ AU VIN

Serves 4   7–10 *minutes at* 15 *lb* (*high*)

25g (1 oz) butter or margarine
4 slices streaky bacon, chopped
4 chicken portions
16 button onions
100g (4 oz) button mushrooms
2 cloves garlic, crushed (optional)
150ml ($\frac{1}{4}$ pint) chicken stock
150ml ($\frac{1}{4}$ pint) dry red wine
1 teaspoon salt
black pepper
1 bay leaf
1 tablespoon cornflour
2 tablespoons brandy

In the open pressure cooker, without the trivet, fry the bacon in the butter until starting to brown. Add the chicken and brown evenly on all sides. Add the onions, mushrooms, garlic (if used), stock, wine, seasoning and bay leaf. Fit the lid and bring to pressure. Cook for 7–10 minutes at 15 lb (high) pressure. Reduce pressure quickly in cold water. Remove the bay leaf. Remove the chicken to a hot serving dish to keep warm. Blend the cornflour with the brandy and pour into the sauce. Bring to the boil, stirring continuously, until thickened. Pour over the chicken to serve.

CHICKEN MARENGO

Serves 4   7–10 *minutes at* 15 *lb* (*high*)

25g (1 oz) butter or margarine
1 onion, chopped

4 chicken portions
4 tomatoes, skinned and quartered
1 clove garlic, crushed (optional)
100g (4 oz) button mushrooms
300ml (½ pint) dry white wine
bouquet garni
1 teaspoon salt
pepper
1 tablespoon cornflour
2 tablespoons brandy

In the open pressure cooker, without the trivet, gently fry the onion in the butter until softened but not browned. Add the chicken portions and brown evenly on all sides. Add the tomatoes, mushrooms, wine, garlic (if used) herbs and seasoning. Fit the lid and bring to pressure. Cook for 7–10 minutes at 15 lb (high) pressure. Reduce pressure quickly in cold water. Using a slotted spoon, remove the chicken to a hot serving dish to keep warm. Blend the cornflour with the brandy and pour into the sauce. Bring to the boil, stirring continuously, until thickened. Pour the sauce over the chicken to serve.

CHICKEN AND LEEK PUDDINGS

Serves 4   15 *minutes pre-steaming*
                              30 *minutes at 5 lb (low)*

100g (4 oz) self-raising flour
50g (2 oz) shredded suet
pinch of salt
pepper
4 tablespoons cold water
25g (1 oz) butter or margarine
4 rashers bacon, chopped
1 onion, finely chopped
2 leeks, finely sliced (use only white part)
1 teaspoon salt
pepper
½ teaspoon thyme
4 chicken thighs

Mix together the flour, suet and seasoning with sufficient cold water to make a firm dough. Cut the pastry into 4 and roll into circles large enough to wrap around each chicken portion. Cut 4 squares of aluminium foil, approximately the same size as the pastry. Grease and lie the pastry on the foil.

In a pan gently fry the bacon in the butter until starting to brown. Add the onion and leeks, cooking gently until softened but not browned. Add seasoning and thyme. Spread this mixture over each pastry circle, and lie the chicken portions on top. Moisten the edges of the pastry and fold over the filling, crimping the edges at the top, rather like a Cornish pasty. Seal the foil loosely but securely around the puddings. Pour 850ml (1½ pints) water into the pressure cooker and add the trivet. Stand the 4 parcels on the trivet, sealed side uppermost. Fit the lid *without* the weight and steam for 15 minutes on a gentle heat. Fit the weight and bring to pressure. Cook for 30 minutes at 5 lb (low) pressure. Reduce pressure slowly at room temperature. Remove the puddings from the foil to serve.

CHICKEN ESPAGNOLE

Serves 4   7–10 *minutes at* 15 *lb* (*high*)

25g (1 oz) butter or margarine
2 rashers streaky bacon, chopped
1 onion, chopped
1 carrot, diced
2 sticks celery, thinly sliced
4 chicken portions
300ml (½ pint) chicken stock
2 tablespoons tomato purée
1 teaspoon salt
pepper
1 tablespoon cornflour
1 tablespoon sherry

In the open pressure cooker, without the trivet, fry the bacon in the butter until it starts to brown. Add the onion, carrot and celery and fry gently until softened but not browned. Add the chicken joints and brown evenly on all sides. Add the stock, purée and seasoning. Fit the lid and bring to pressure. Cook for 7–10 minutes at 15 lb (high) pressure. Reduce pressure quickly in cold water. Remove the chicken to a hot serving dish to keep warm. Strain the sauce into a clean pan. Blend the cornflour with sherry and pour into the sauce. Bring to the boil, stirring continuously until thickened. Pour over the chicken to serve.

HOT NUTTY CHICKEN

Serves 4   7–10 *minutes at* 15 *lb* (high)

2 tablespoons oil
1 onion, sliced
1 clove garlic, crushed (optional)
1 teaspoon chilli powder
1 teaspoon ground ginger
1 tablespoon curry powder
4 chicken portions, skinned
300ml ($\frac{1}{2}$ pint) chicken stock
3 tablespoons natural yoghurt
100g (4 oz) cashew nuts

In the open pressure cooker, without the trivet, gently fry the onion and garlic (if used) in the oil until softened, but not browned. Add the chilli powder, ginger and curry powder, and cook over a low heat for 2 minutes. Stir in the chicken stock and add the chicken portions. Fit the lid and bring to pressure. Cook for 7–10 minutes at 15 lb (high) pressure. Reduce pressure quickly in cold water. Remove from the heat and just before serving stir in the yoghurt and nuts. Do not re-heat.

If cooking this dish in advance to freeze or re-heat the next day, do not add the yoghurt or nuts until just before serving.

CHICKEN WITH HERB DUMPLINGS

Serves 4   7 *minutes at* 15 *lb* (high)
                                              10 *minutes steaming*

25g (1 oz) butter or margarine
1 onion, sliced
1 carrot, sliced
6 sticks of celery, sliced
4 chicken portions

Chicken with Herb Dumplings contd.

1 teaspoon salt
pepper
300ml (½ pint) chicken stock
50g (2 oz) self-raising flour
25g (1 oz) shredded suet
½ teaspoon salt
pepper
1 teaspoon dried mixed herbs
2 teaspoons cold water

In the open pressure cooker, without the trivet, gently fry the onion and celery in the butter until softened but not browned. Add the chicken, and brown evenly on all sides. Add the carrots, seasoning and stock. Fit the lid and bring to pressure. Cook for 7 minutes at 15 lb (high) pressure. Reduce pressure quickly in cold water. While the chicken is cooking, mix together the flour, suet, seasoning and herbs with sufficient water to make a firm dough. Shape into 8 balls and add to the pressure cooker. Fit the lid *without* the weight and steam on a gentle heat for 10 minutes.

DUCK A L'ORANGE

Serves 4   12 *minutes at* 15 *lb* (*high*)

As duck tends to be rather fatty, it is better if this dish can be prepared a day ahead. In this case, do not thicken or add the Cointreau until the re-heating stage, and only cook for 8 minutes. When cold remove the fat from the surface. To re-heat, cook at 15 lb (high) pressure for 4 minutes. Reduce pressure quickly in cold water and add the thickening and Cointreau.

25g (1 oz) butter or margarine
1 duck, divided into 4 joints
1 onion, chopped
1 teaspoon salt
pepper
grated rind 1 orange
juice 2 oranges
300ml (½ pint) chicken stock
2 tablespoons cornflour
2 tablespoons Cointreau

In the open pressure cooker, without the trivet, brown the duck joints in the butter on all sides. Remove the joints and drain away the remaining fat. Return the joints to the pressure cooker and add the onion, seasoning, orange rind and juice. Add the stock, fit the lid and bring to pressure. Cook for 12 minutes at 15 lb (high) pressure. Reduce pressure quickly in cold water. Remove the joints to a hot serving dish and keep warm. Skim the fat. Blend the cornflour with the Cointreau and pour into the sauce. Bring to the boil, stirring continuously until thickened. Pour over the duck and serve.

PHEASANT AND GRAPE CASSEROLE

Serves 4   7–10 *minutes at* 15 *lb* (*high*)

25g (1 oz) butter or margarine
1 large or 2 small pheasants
1 onion, finely chopped
2 sticks celery, thinly sliced
150ml ($\frac{1}{4}$ pint) stock
150ml ($\frac{1}{4}$ pint) dry white wine
bouquet garni
1 teaspoon salt
black pepper
225g (8 oz) green grapes, peeled, halved and de-seeded
4 tablespoons double cream

In the open pressure cooker, without the trivet, brown the pheasant(s) in the butter on all sides, turning frequently for even colouring. Remove from the pressure cooker and drain away the remaining fat. Place the onion and celery in the pressure cooker and add the pheasant, stock, wine, bouquet garni, salt and pepper. Fit the lid and bring to pressure. Cook for 7–10 minutes (the latter if you have one large pheasant) at 15 lb (high) pressure. Reduce pressure quickly in cold water. Remove the bouquet garni. Add the grapes and heat through on a gentle heat. Remove from the heat and stir in the cream just before serving.

RAGOÛT OF VENISON

Serves 4   30 *minutes at* 15 *lb* (*high*)

1 onion, finely chopped
1 teaspoon salt
6 black peppercorns, crushed
1 bay leaf
6 tablespoons oil
3 tablespoons dry red wine
1kg (2 lb) venison, cubed
25g (1 oz) butter or margarine
4 rashers streaky, bacon, chopped
2 onions, chopped
2 carrots, chopped
300ml ($\frac{1}{2}$ pint) dry red wine
bouquet garni
$\frac{1}{2}$ teaspoon salt
black pepper
2 tablespoons cornflour

Mix together the onion, salt, peppercorns, bay leaf, oil and 3 tablespoons of dry red wine. Steep the venison in this marinade for 2 hours. In the open pressure cooker, without the trivet, fry the bacon in the butter until starting to brown. Remove the venison from the marinade and pat dry. Brown the venison on all sides and add the onions, carrots, 300ml ($\frac{1}{2}$ pint) wine, bouquet garni, salt and pepper. Fit the lid and bring to pressure. Cook for 30 minutes at 15 lb (high) pressure. Reduce pressure quickly in cold water. Remove the bouquet garni. Blend the cornflour with the strained marinade and add to the ragoût. Bring to the boil, stirring continuously until thickened.

JUGGED HARE

Serves 4   35 *minutes at* 15 *lb* (*high*)

25g (1 oz) butter or margarine
2 rashers streaky bacon, chopped

1 hare, jointed (reserve blood if wished)
1 onion, chopped
2 carrots, sliced
2 sticks celery, sliced
1 teaspoon salt
black pepper
bouquet garni
425ml (¾ pint) stock or water
1 tablespoon lemon juice
1 tablespoon cornflour
1 tablespoon water
1 tablespoon redcurrant jelly
4 tablespoons port

In the open pressure cooker, without the trivet, fry the bacon in the butter until beginning to brown. Add the hare and brown on all sides. Add the vegetables, seasoning, bouquet garni, stock or water and lemon juice. Fit the lid and bring to pressure. Cook for 35 minutes at 15 lb (high) pressure. Reduce pressure quickly with cold water. Mix the cornflour with the water and pour into the pressure cooker. Bring to the boil, stirring continuously until thickened. Remove from the heat and stir in the port, jelly and, if wished, the blood. Do not re-heat once the blood has been added.

RABBIT AND PRUNE CASSEROLE

Serves 4   *20–25 minutes at 15 lb (high)*

100g (4 oz) dried prunes
25g (1 oz) butter or margarine
1 onion, sliced
1kg (2 lb) rabbit joints, washed in salted water, rinsed and dried
25g (1 oz) flour
225g (8 oz) carrots, sliced
425ml (¾ pint) chicken stock or soaking water from prunes
1 teaspoon salt
pepper
bay leaf

Leave the prunes to soak in 300ml ($\frac{1}{2}$ pint) boiling water for 10 minutes. In the open pressure cooker, without the trivet, gently fry the onion until softened but not browned. Toss the rabbit in the flour and brown on all sides in the pressure cooker. Stir in all the remaining ingredients, fit the lid and bring to pressure. Cook for 20–25 minutes at 15 lb (high) pressure. Reduce pressure quickly with cold water. Remove the bayleaf before serving.

PIGEON CASSEROLE

Serves 4   25–30 *minutes at* 15 *lb* (*high*)

4 wood pigeons
25g (1 oz) butter or margarine
1 onion, sliced
4 carrots, sliced
2 parsnips, sliced
2 sticks celery, sliced
1 bay leaf
300ml ($\frac{1}{2}$ pint) stock
1 teaspoon salt
pepper
1 tablespoon cornflour
1 tablespoon water

Skin the pigeons and remove the wings, legs and breast. If wished, the rinsed carcass can be used to make the stock. In the open pressure cooker, without the trivet, fry the pigeon meat in the butter until browned on all sides. Add the vegetables, bay leaf, seasoning and stock. Fit the lid and bring to pressure. Cook for 25–30 minutes at 15 lb (high) pressure. Reduce pressure quickly in cold water. Remove the bay leaf. Blend the cornflour with the water and pour into the casserole. Bring to the boil, stirring continuously, until thickened.

TURKEY À LA CRÈME

Serves 4   20 *minutes altogether at* 15 *lb* (*high*)

25g (1 oz) butter or margarine
4 turkey portions
1 teaspoon salt
black pepper
300ml (½ pint) stock
bouquet garni
16 button onions, peeled
100g (4 oz) button mushrooms
1 tablespoon cornflour
1 tablespoon water
2 egg yolks, beaten
4 tablespoons double cream
1 tablespoon lemon juice

In the open pressure cooker, without the trivet, brown the turkey portions in the butter on all sides. Add the seasoning, bouquet garni and stock. Fit the lid and bring to pressure. Cook for 15 minutes at 15 lb (high) pressure. Reduce pressure quickly in cold water. Add the onions and mushrooms, fit the lid and bring to pressure. Cook for a further 5 minutes at 15 lb (high) pressure. Reduce pressure quickly in cold water. Remove the bouquet garni. Blend the cornflour with the water. Pour into the pressure cooker and bring to the boil stirring continuously until thickened. Mix the egg yolks with the lemon juice and cream and add to this mixture 3 tablespoons of the sauce. With the pressure cooker on a low heat, pour this mixture into the sauce and stir until thickened. Do not allow the sauce to boil.

5

FISH

Time saving is not the big advantage when pressure cooking fish; indeed, conventional methods don't take much longer. The main advantage is that only the minimum liquid is usually required and this helps reduce loss of flavour. Furthermore, the strong smell of fish is trapped inside the pressure cooker until the end of cooking.

A good source of protein, fish is available 'wet' from fishmongers or ready-prepared from the frozen food cabinet. There are advantages in buying from either. Frozen fish doesn't need time spent in its preparation and is guaranteed fresh when frozen. On the other hand, the skin, bones, head and fins of whole fish make the basis of a stock which will improve most fish recipes.

The following cooking methods can be adapted to pressure cooking.

Poaching
The trivet is not used.

The fish is prepared and placed in the pressure cooker.

A minimum of 300ml ($\frac{1}{2}$ pint) liquid is added. This may be lightly salted water with a teaspoon of lemon juice, or wine or cider. If the poaching liquid is to be used as the basis of a sauce, sliced vegetables and herbs may be included to give extra flavour. A mixture of half milk to water is recommended for smoked fish and no salt should be added.

Fit the lid and bring to 15 lb (high) pressure. Cook for the time recommended in the table overleaf.

Reduce pressure quickly in cold water.

The fish may then be flaked and served in a sauce, pie, flan, pancakes or vol au vent cases. If the fish is to be served cold, it should be allowed to cool in the poaching liquor.

Steaming
The trivet is used and should be greased to prevent the fish from sticking.

Put a minumum of 300ml ($\frac{1}{2}$ pint) water into the pressure cooker with the trivet. Ensure that the water level is no higher than the trivet.

Prepare the fish and place it on the trivet. Sprinkle with lemon juice, salt and pepper.

Fit the lid and bring to 15 lb (high) pressure. Cook for the time recommended in the table.

Reduce pressure quickly in cold water.

En papillote
The trivet is used.

The fish should be prepared and placed on a greased square of aluminium foil. It may be seasoned and dotted with butter, stuffed or sprinkled with finely sliced vegetables such as onion, mushrooms or celery. The foil should then be folded to form a parcel.

Put 300ml (½ pint) water into the pressure cooker with the trivet.

Place the parcel on the trivet, fit the lid and bring to 15 lb (high) pressure. Cook for the time recommended in the table.

Reduce pressure quickly in cold water.

Stewing

The trivet is not used.

The fish is prepared and cut into chunks.

An onion and other vegetables may be sautéed in butter or margarine in the open pressure cooker. As fish takes such a short time to pressure cook, ensure that root vegetables, such as potatoes and carrots, are thinly sliced to cook within the same time.

Add the fish, lemon juice and at least 300ml (½ pint) of stock, wine or cider. Add herbs and seasoning.

Fit the lid and bring to 15 lb (high) pressure. Cook for the time recommended in the table.

Reduce pressure quickly in cold water.

Braising

Follow the general method for stewing, except that the fish is cooked whole on the buttered trivet, which is placed on top of the vegetables and raised above the liquid. The vegetables may be puréed afterwards to make the sauce.

Cooking times

	Steaks or fillets	Whole
Bass, bream, brill, cod, coley, haddock, hake, halibut, ling, plaice, skate, sole, turbot, whiting	3–6 minutes	5–6 minutes per 450g (1 lb)
Herrings, mackerel, mullet, trout		5–8 minutes
Salmon		8–12 minutes per 450g (1 lb)
Lobster		10 minutes
Crab		7–10 minutes
Prawns, shrimps		2–3 minutes

Times will vary depending on the thickness of the fish.

Frozen fish
There is no need to thaw frozen fish before cooking, unless it is to be stuffed. Cooking times are the same as for fresh fish.

Greasing
In some of the recipes it is necessary to grease the trivet, foil or dish, etc., and this can be done with butter, margarine or lard, according to taste.

SMOKY KEDGEREE

Serves 4   8 *minutes at* 15 *lb* (*high*)

This is a tasty variation of the traditional recipe and uses smoked mackerel which doesn't need separate cooking in advance.

4 eggs
450g (1 lb) smoked mackerel fillets
25g (1 oz) butter or margarine
1 small onion, chopped
175g (6 oz) long grain rice
550ml (1 pint) stock or water
2 tablespoons cream or top of the milk

In a small saucepan, boil the eggs for 10 minutes until hard. Flake the fish, removing bones and skin which may be used to make the stock. In the open pressure cooker, without the trivet, gently fry the onion in the butter until softened, but not browned. Add the rice and stir over a low heat for a couple of minutes. Add the stock or water and bring to the boil, stirring continuously. Reduce the heat to a medium setting, fit the lid and bring to pressure on this heat. Cook for 8 minutes at 15 lb (high) pressure. Reduce pressure slowly at room temperature. Chop the hard boiled eggs and stir into the rice together with the fish. Add the cream or milk and stir gently over a low heat until piping hot.

STUFFED PLAICE IN ORANGE

Serves 4   8 *minutes at* 15 *lb* (high)

8 small fillets of plaice
1 orange (grated rind and half the juice)
50g (2 oz) fresh breadcrumbs
1 teaspoon dill
1 teaspoon salt
pepper
300ml ($\frac{1}{2}$ pint) orange juice
1 tablespoon cornflour

Mix together the orange rind, half the juice from the orange, breadcrumbs, dill and seasoning. Divide the stuffing equally between the fillets and spread over the skin side of each one. Roll up the fillets from the thinnest end and secure with a cocktail stick. Reserve a tablespoon from the $\frac{1}{2}$ pint of orange juice to blend with the cornflour and pour the remainder into the pressure cooker, without the trivet. Arrange the rolled fillets in the pressure cooker, fit the lid and bring to pressure. Cook for 8 minutes at 15 lb (high) pressure. Reduce pressure quickly in cold water. Blend the orange juice with the cornflour. Using a slotted spoon, remove the fish to a serving dish and remove the cocktail sticks. Add the blended cornflour to the sauce and bring to the boil, stirring continuously until thickened. Season if necessary and pour over the fish to serve.

TUNA SOUFFLÉ

Serves 4   15 *minutes at* 10 *lb* (medium)

Please note that this recipe is cooked at 10 lb (medium) pressure to allow it to rise.

150ml ($\frac{1}{4}$ pint) milk
212g ($7\frac{1}{2}$ oz) can tuna, drained and flaked
100g (4 oz) fresh breadcrumbs
1 teaspoon salt
black pepper
2 teaspoons parsley, chopped
4 eggs, separated

Put 300ml ($\frac{1}{2}$ pint) water into the pressure cooker and add the trivet. Grease a 1 litre (2 pint) soufflé dish. In a small pan heat the milk until lukewarm. Mix the milk with the tuna, breadcrumbs, seasoning and parsley, and beat in the 4 egg yolks. Whisk the egg whites until stiff and gently fold into the fish mixture. Put the mixture into the soufflé dish and cover securely with a piece of buttered aluminium foil. Stand the soufflé on the trivet, fit the lid and bring to pressure. Cook for 15 minutes at 10 lb (medium) pressure. Reduce pressure slowly at room temperature and serve immediately.

COD PROVENÇALE

Serves 4   4 *minutes at* 15 *lb* (*high*)

25g (1 oz) butter or margarine
1 onion, finely chopped
1 clove garlic, crushed (optional)
700g (1$\frac{1}{2}$ lb) cod, cut into 4 portions
397g (14 oz) can tomatoes
1 green pepper, de-seeded and chopped
1 tablespoon tomato purée
$\frac{1}{2}$ teaspoon brown sugar
1 bay leaf
1 teaspoon salt
pepper
1 teaspoon parsley, chopped

In the open pressure cooker, without the trivet, gently fry the onion in the butter until softened but not browned. Add the garlic, if wished, and the remaining ingredients, except the parsley. Fit the lid and bring to pressure. Cook for 4 minutes at 15 lb (high) pressure. Reduce pressure quickly with cold water. Remove the bay leaf before serving and sprinkle with parsley.

APPLE MACKEREL

Serves 4   10 *minutes at* 15 *lb* (*high*)

This is quite a filling dish, so choose 4 smallish mackerel or divide two large ones.

4 mackerel
25g (1 oz) butter or margarine
1 onion, finely chopped
2 cooking apples, peeled, cored and finely chopped
50g (2 oz) fresh breadcrumbs
50g (2 oz) grated cheese
1 teaspoon salt
pepper

Clean the mackerel and remove the head, fins and back-bone. Rinse and wipe dry. In a small pan gently fry the onion in the butter until softened but not browned. Add the apple and fry for a further minute. Remove from the heat and mix with the breadcrumbs, cheese and seasoning. Divide the stuffing equally between the 4 fish and spread inside. Close the fish and place on 4 squares of greased aluminium foil. Fold securely to make 4 parcels. Put 300ml (½ pint) water into the pressure cooker with the trivet. Stand the parcels on the trivet, fit the lid and bring to pressure. Cook for 10 minutes at 15 lb (high) pressure. Reduce pressure quickly in cold water. Remove the fish from the foil to serve.

DEVON FISH CASSEROLE

Serves 4   4 *minutes at* 15 *lb (high)*

25g (1 oz) butter or margarine
1 onion, finely chopped
450g (1 lb) whiting, cut into chunks
225g (8 oz) prawns, peeled weight, or thawed
225g (8 oz) mushrooms, sliced
juice ½ lemon
300ml (½ pint) dry cider
1 teaspoon salt
pepper
pinch thyme
150ml (¼ pint) double cream

In the open pressure cooker, without the trivet, gently fry the onion in the butter until softened but not browned. Add the fish, prawns, mushrooms, lemon juice, cider, seasoning and thyme. Fit the lid and bring to pressure. Cook for 4 minutes at 15 lb (high) pressure. Reduce pressure quickly in cold water. Pour the cream into the casserole and heat gently on a low setting. Do not allow to boil.

FISHERMAN'S PUDDING

Serves 4   15 *minutes steaming*
                                              25 *minutes at 5 lb (low)*

212g (7½ oz) can salmon, drained and flaked
1 small onion, finely chopped
225g (8 oz) mashed potato (use dried potato for speed)
50g (2 oz) fresh breadcrumbs
1 tablespoon chopped fresh chives
1 egg, beaten
2 tablespoons milk
50g (2 oz) melted butter
1 teaspoon Worcestershire Sauce
1 teaspoon salt
pepper

Grease a 1 litre (2 pint) pudding basin. Mix together all the ingredients and put into the basin. Cover securely with a double layer of greaseproof paper or aluminium foil. Put 850ml (1½ pints) water into the pressure cooker with the trivet. Stand the basin on the trivet, fit the lid *without* the weight, and steam for 15 minutes on a gentle heat. Fit the weight and bring to pressure. Cook for 25 minutes at 5 lb (low) pressure. Reduce pressure slowly at room temperature. Serve from the basin.

TROUT WITH ALMONDS

Serves 4   8 *minutes at 15 lb (high)*

4 trout
salt
pepper
1 tablespoon lemon juice
100g (4 oz) butter
50g (2 oz) flaked almonds

Clean the trout and remove the heads. Dry and place on 4 greased squares of aluminium foil. Sprinkle each trout with lemon juice and seasoning. In a small pan fry the almonds in the butter until slightly brown and pour both over the trout. Fold the foil over the trout to make 4 sealed parcels. Put 300ml (½ pint) water into the pressure cooker with the trivet. Lie the parcels on the trivet, fit the lid and bring to pressure. Cook for 8 minutes at 15 lb (high) pressure. Reduce pressure quickly in cold water. Remove from the foil to serve.

CHEESY FISH PIE

Serves 4   3 *minutes at* 15 *lb* (*high*)

1 onion, finely chopped
1 carrot, finely diced
700g (1½ lb) white fish such as cod, whiting, coley
100g (4 oz) grated cheese
225g (8 oz) tomatoes, skinned and sliced
150ml (¼ pint) fish stock or water
1 teaspoon salt
pepper
2 tablespoons cornflour
75ml (⅛ pint) milk
75g (3 oz) fresh breadcrumbs

Grease the base of the pressure cooker. Sprinkle the onion and carrots over the base of the pressure cooker, without the trivet. Cut the fish into chunks and place on top of the vegetables. Sprinkle with cheese, reserving 25g (1 oz) for the topping, and cover with the tomatoes. Season and cover with the stock or water. Fit the lid and bring to pressure. Cook for 3 minutes at 15 lb (high) pressure. Reduce pressure quickly in cold water. Using a slotted spoon, remove the fish and tomatoes to an oven-proof serving dish, to keep warm. Blend the cornflour with the milk and add to the sauce in the pressure cooker. Bring to the boil, stirring until thickened. Pour over the fish, sprinkle with cheese and breadcrumb mixture and brown under the grill.

SOUSED HERRINGS

Serves 4   6 *minutes at* 15 *lb (high)*

8 small herrings
1 tablespoon salt
black pepper
1 blade mace
8 black peppercorns
2 small onions, thinly sliced
1 bay leaf
150ml (¼ pint) malt vinegar
150ml (¼ pint) water

Clean the herrings and remove the head, tail and fins of each. Split in half and remove the bones. Sprinkle the inside of each half with salt and pepper. Roll up the fillets from the tail end, with the skin side outwards. Secure with cocktail sticks and put into the pressure cooker without the trivet. Add the remaining ingredients, fit the lid and bring to pressure. Cook for 6 minutes at 15 lb (high) pressure. Reduce pressure quickly in cold water. Remove the cocktail sticks from the herrings and place the fish in a china or glass serving dish. Pour the liquid over the herrings, decorate with the onion, bay leaf and peppercorns, and allow to cool before serving.

SALMON SAVOURY

Serves 4   15 *minutes at* 15 *lb (high)*

50g (2 oz) long grain rice, cooked
212g (7½ oz) can salmon, drained and flaked
1 small onion, finely chopped
1 tablespoon parsley, chopped
2 eggs, beaten
150ml (¼ pint) milk, warmed
½ teaspoon salt
1 teaspoon cayenne pepper

Grease 4 individual oven-proof dishes or breakfast cups. Mix together all the dry ingredients and divide between the dishes. Mix together the milk and eggs and pour over the salmon mixture. Cover securely with aluminium foil. Put

550ml (1 pint) water into the pressure cooker with the trivet. Stand the dishes on the trivet, fit the lid and bring to pressure. The dishes should not touch the sides of the pressure cooker as they could crack. If they don't all fit in easily, cook in two batches. Cook for 15 minutes at 15 lb (high) pressure. Reduce pressure slowly at room temperature. Allow to cool and chill before turning out.

WHITING IN CAPER SAUCE

Serves 4   *4 minutes at 15 lb (high)*

700g (1½ lb) whiting fillets, skinned
1 onion, finely chopped
3 teaspoons capers
1 teaspoon salt
black pepper
150ml (¼ pint) fish stock or water
150ml (¼ pint) milk
1 tablespoon cornflour
1 tablespoon milk

Sprinkle the onion over the base of the pressure cooker, without the trivet. Add the fish and sprinkle with capers and seasoning. Add the stock or water and milk. Fit the lid and bring to pressure. Cook for 4 minutes at 15 lb (high) pressure. Reduce pressure quickly in cold water. Blend the milk and cornflour. Using a slotted spoon, remove the fish to a serving dish to keep warm. Add the blended cornflour to the sauce and bring to the boil, stirring continuously until thickened. Pour over the fish and serve.

MACKEREL WITH GOOSEBERRY SAUCE

Serves 4   *8 minutes at 15 lb (high)*

The slightly sharp gooseberry sauce complements the rather rich flavour of the mackerel.

4 small mackerel, cleaned and with heads removed
25g (1 oz) melted butter
1 teaspoon lemon juice

salt
pepper
225g (8 oz) gooseberries
4 tablespoons water
pinch of nutmeg
25g (1 oz) caster sugar

Grease 4 squares of aluminium foil. Brush the insides of the mackerel with the butter. Sprinkle with lemon juice, salt and pepper. Wrap each mackerel in the foil to make 4 sealed parcels. Put the gooseberries, nutmeg and water into an unperforated separator basket or container. Cover securely with aluminium foil. Put 300ml ($\frac{1}{2}$ pint) water into the pressure cooker, with the trivet. Stand the container on the trivet with the 4 parcels. Fit the lid, ensuring that none of the parcels block any air vents. Bring to pressure and cook for 8 minutes at 15 lb (high) pressure. Reduce pressure quickly in cold water. Add the sugar to the gooseberries, while still hot, and stir until the sugar dissolves. Blend the gooseberries in a liquidizer until smooth or mash with a fork for a coarser sauce. Remove the fish from the foil to serve. Pour over the sauce or serve in a sauce boat.

6

VEGETABLES

Vegetables benefit from pressure cooking not only because it saves time, but also because it reduces the loss of colour and vitamins which occurs when cooking in a pan of boiling water. Some colour and flavour is absorbed by the steam and retained, instead of being lost, and the small amount of cooking water used can be added to flavour soups or gravy.

All in together

A selection of vegetables may be pressure cooked simultaneously, but ideally they should have similar cooking times otherwise the more delicate vegetables over-cook. If this is not possible then the larger vegetables should be cut smaller. Medium sized potatoes can cook within the same time as whole carrots and parsnips, but if sliced carrots are preferred, the other vegetables should be cut smaller. Mashed potatoes, carrots and runner beans can be cooked at the same time by finely slicing the potato, thinly slicing the carrots and leaving the beans in fairly large lengths.

Cooking times

The cooking times of vegetables are given on page 85 and should be used as a guide, as the size and quality of vegetables will influence the length of time. For example, whole carrots take longer to cook than when sliced; new potatoes need longer than old ones. Individual taste also varies, so if you prefer your vegetables with a 'bite', reduce the time by about a minute.

Main course vegetables

As meat becomes increasingly expensive more people are eating a main course containing little or no meat. Some of the following recipes are intended as a main course and some could be either main course or side vegetable. In the latter case the servings are shown as 4 *or* 2, to indicate that the quantity is sufficient for two main course helpings.

Fresh vegetables

The trivet is used to keep the vegetables above the water. Use the minimum amount of liquid required; either 300ml ($\frac{1}{2}$ pint) or 150ml ($\frac{1}{4}$ pint).

Prepare the vegetables and put into the perforated baskets, which are stood on the trivet. If a large quantity of only one vegetable is being cooked, it may be piled on to the trivet, only up to two thirds full, without the need for the baskets.

Fit the lid and bring to pressure. Cook at 15 lb (high) pressure for the time recommended in the table.

Reduce pressure quickly in cold water.

Dried vegetables

Dried beans and peas, etc., have become more popular as an alternative source of protein to meat. With a pressure cooker long overnight soaking is unnecessary. Lentils require no soaking at all and the remaining vegetables need only an hour.

Wash the dried vegetables, cover with boiling water and leave to soak for an hour. Do not use bicarbonate of soda, as it will stain the pressure cooker.

The trivet is not required. Pour into the pressure cooker at least 1 litre (2 pints) liquid, part of which can be made up from the soaking water. This quantity is sufficient for cooking 450g (1 lb) of vegetables and should be increased proportionally if more vegetables are to be cooked.

Bring the liquid to the boil and add the drained vegetables. Don't fill the pressure cooker more than half full of vegetables and liquid as they tend to froth up during cooking.

Reduce the heat to a medium setting, fit the lid and bring to pressure on this heat. Cook at 15 lb (high) pressure for the recommended time in the table.

Reduce pressure slowly at room temperature.

Blanching for freezing

Blanching in a pressure cooker is quicker, uses less fuel and reduces the steam in the kitchen. Instead of the large pan of boiling water usually needed, you only require the minimum amount recommended for your pressure cooker, either 300ml ($\frac{1}{2}$ pint) or 150ml ($\frac{1}{4}$ pint).

Follow this basic method, ensuring that the recommended time is not exceeded, otherwise the vegetables will be cooked rather than blanched.

Prepare the vegetables for freezing, as you would normally.

Put the water into the pressure cooker, together with the trivet, and bring the water to the boil.

Pile the vegetables loosely into the perforated baskets or a special blanching basket. Don't fill the pressure cooker more than two thirds full or pack the vegetables too tightly, as this prevents full circulation of the steam.

Fit the lid and bring to 10 lb (medium) pressure. Follow the table for blanching times.

Reduce pressure quickly in cold water. Remove the vegetables and plunge them into cold water to cool quickly. Drain, dry, pack and freeze as usual.

When pressure cooking frozen vegetables, do not thaw but cook for the time recommended for fresh vegetables.

Cooking times for dried vegetables

	Minutes
Butter beans	30
Haricot beans, small	20
Haricot beans, large	30
Kidney beans	20
Lentils	7
Peas, whole	20
Peas, split	15

Cooking times for fresh vegetables

	Minutes
Artichokes, globe	6–10
Artichokes, Jerusalem	4–6
Asparagus	2–4
Beans, broad	3–5
Beans, French or runner	3–5
Beetroot, small	10
medium	15–20
large	20–30
Broccoli	3–4
Brussels sprouts	3–4
Cabbage, shredded	3
Carrots, whole	6–7
sliced	3–4
Cauliflower, whole	5–8
florets	3–4
Celery	3
Chicory, whole	3–6
Courgettes, whole	3–4
sliced	2
Leeks, whole	4
sliced	2
Marrow, thickly sliced	3–4
Onions, sliced	3
whole	6–10
Parsnips, quartered	5–7
sliced	4
Peas	3–4
Peppers, stuffed	5
Potatoes, new, small, whole	6–7
old, whole	12
old, quartered	7
old, sliced	5
Spinach	1–2
Swede, cubed	4
Sweet corn, whole	3–5
Turnip, sliced	3–5

Blanching times (*Pressure* 10 *lb* (*medium*))
Minutes

Artichokes, Jerusalem, cubed	1
Asparagus	only to pressure
Beans, broad	1
Beans, French or runner	only to pressure
Beetroot, sliced	7
Broccoli	1
Brussels sprouts	1
Carrots	2
Cauliflower, florets	1
Celery, young hearts	2
sticks	1
Courgettes, sliced	1
Chicory	1
Parsnips, sliced	1
Peas	1
Potatoes, new small	2
Spinach	only to pressure
Swedes, sliced	1
Sweet corn	2
Turnips, small, whole	2

RATATOUILLE

Serves 4 or 2 5 *minutes at* 15 *lb* (*high*)

1 tablespoon olive oil
1 onion, chopped
1 clove garlic, crushed
2 green peppers, de-seeded and sliced
1 aubergine, sliced
4 courgettes, thickly sliced
450g (1 lb) tomatoes, skinned and quartered
1 teaspoon salt
pepper
150ml (¼ pint) water

In the open pressure cooker, without the trivet, gently fry the onion and garlic until softened but not browned. Add the remaining ingredients, fit the lid and bring to pressure. Cook for 5 minutes at 15 lb (high) pressure. Reduce pressure quickly in cold water.

CREAMY CABBAGE

Serves 4 or 2   *4 minutes at* 15 *lb* (*high*)

25g (1 oz) butter or margarine
1 onion, finely chopped
1 small or ½ a large white cabbage, finely shredded
150ml (¼ pint) chicken stock
1 teaspoon salt
pepper
pinch nutmeg
1 tablespoon cornflour
150ml (¼ pint) milk

In the open pressure cooker, without the trivet, gently fry
the onion in the butter until softened but not browned. Add
the cabbage, stock and seasoning, mixing well together. Fit
the lid and bring to pressure. Cook for 4 minutes at 15 lb
(high) pressure. Reduce pressure quickly in cold water.
Blend together the milk and cornflour to make a smooth
cream. Stir into the cabbage and bring to the boil, stirring
continuously, until thickened.

COURGETTES PROVENÇALES

Serves 4 or 2   *4 minutes at* 15 *lb* (*high*)

1 tablespoon olive oil
1 onion, sliced
1 clove garlic, crushed
1kg (2 lb) courgettes, cut in 10mm (½ in) slices
227g (8 oz) can of tomatoes, including juice
1 teaspoon salt
freshly ground black pepper
pinch of mixed herbs

In the open pressure cooker, without the trivet, gently fry
the onion and garlic in the oil until softened but not browned.
Add the remaining ingredients, fit the lid and bring to pressure. Cook for 4 minutes at 15 lb (high) pressure. Reduce
pressure quickly in cold water.

BEANS AMERICAN STYLE

Serves 4   30 *minutes at* 15 *lb* (*high*)

This makes a tasy and filling main course dish. It is easier to eat if served in a soup bowl.

450g (1 lb) dried butter beans
1 litre (2 pints) boiling water
25g (1 oz) butter or margarine
100g (4 oz) streaky bacon, chopped
1 onion, chopped
297g (14 oz) can of tomatoes, including juice
1 chicken stock cube
2 tablespoons tomato purée
1 teaspoon salt
pepper
bay leaf
1 tablespoon lemon juice

Wash the beans and soak for an hour in boiling water. In the open pressure cooker, without the trivet, fry the bacon in the butter until starting to brown. Add the onion and gently fry until softened but not browned. Drain the beans (reserving the soaking liquid) and add to the pressure cooker. Pour the whole can of tomatoes into a measuring jug, and make the amount up to 1 litre (1¾ pints) using some of the soaking liquid. Add this to the pressure cooker, together with the remaining ingredients. Bring to the boil then reduce the heat to medium. Fit the lid and bring to pressure on this heat. Cook for 30 minutes at 15 lb (high) pressure. Reduce pressure slowly at room temperature. Remove the bay leaf and serve.

GERMAN RED CABBAGE

Serves 4   4 *minutes at* 15 *lb* (*high*)

This recipe freezes well and is a tangy, alternative vegetable to serve with the turkey on Christmas Day.

25g (1 oz) butter or margarine
1 onion, finely chopped
1 small or ½ a large red cabbage, finely shredded

2 cooking apples, peeled, cored and thickly sliced
25g (1 oz) sultanas
2 tablespoons wine vinegar
2 tablespoons water
1 tablespoon brown sugar
1 teaspoon salt
pepper

In the open pressure cooker, without the trivet, gently fry the onion until softened, but not browned. Add the remaining ingredients and mix well together. Fit the lid and bring to pressure. Cook for 4 minutes at 15 lb (high) pressure. Reduce pressure quickly in cold water.

STUFFED ONIONS

Serves 4   *7 minutes at 15 lb (high)*

4 large onions
25g (1 oz) butter or margarine
225g (8 oz) pork sausage-meat
1 teaspoon dried sage
½ teaspoon salt
pepper
300ml (½ pint) beef stock
1 tablespoon cornflour
1 tablespoon water

Peel the onions, cut a slice from the top and scoop out the centre, leaving a wall two layers thick. Finely chop a third of the removed onion and reserve the remainder for soups or casseroles. In a small pan gently fry the chopped onion in the butter until softened but not browned. Remove with a slotted spoon and mix well with the sausage-meat, sage and seasoning. Fill the onions with this mixture and stand in the pressure cooker, without the trivet. Pour in the stock, fit the lid and bring to pressure. Cook for 7 minutes at 15 lb (high) pressure. Reduce pressure quickly in cold water, taking care not to tip the pressure cooker, causing the onions to fall over. Remove the onions to a serving dish, using two spoons. Blend together the cornflour and water to make a smooth mixture. Pour into the stock and bring to the boil, stirring continuously until thickened. Pour over the onions and serve.

DIJON LENTILS

Serves 4 or 2   *7 minutes at 15 lb (high)*

225g (8 oz) lentils
550ml (1 pint) beef stock
1 onion, chopped
bouquet garni
1 teaspoon salt
pepper
100g (4 oz) ham, cut into strips
1 teaspoon made mustard

Wash the lentils and put into the pressure cooker. Add the stock, onion, seasoning and bouquet garni. Bring to the boil and reduce the heat to a medium setting. Fit the lid and bring to pressure on this heat. Cook for 7 minutes at 15 lb (high) pressure. Reduce pressure slowly at room temperature. Remove the bouquet garni, add the ham and mustard, and heat through, stirring continuously.

SWEETCORN SUPPER POT

Serves 4   *25 minutes at 15 lb (high)*

1 green pepper, de-seeded and finely chopped
326g (11½ oz) can sweetcorn, drained
100g (4 oz) grated cheese
1 pinch sage
1 teaspoon salt
black pepper
300ml (½ pint) milk, warmed
3 eggs, beaten

Mix together all the dry ingredients and seasoning, reserving a little cheese for topping later. Put into a greased 1 litre (2 pint) oven-proof bowl or soufflé dish. Mix the milk with the eggs and pour into the dish. Cover securely with a double layer of greaseproof paper or aluminium foil. Put 550ml (1 pint) water into the pressure cooker with the trivet. Stand the dish on the trivet, fit the lid and bring to pressure. Cook for 25 minutes at 15 lb (high) pressure. Reduce pressure slowly at room temperature. Sprinkle the dish with remaining cheese and brown under the grill.

STUFFED GREEN PEPPERS

Serves 4   *7 minutes at* 15 *lb* (*high*)

Choose peppers of equal size, with flattish bottoms so that they will stand upright during cooking.

25g (1 oz) butter or margarine
1 onion, finely chopped
450g (1 lb) lean minced beef
100g (4 oz) cooked rice
½ teaspoon mixed herbs
1 teaspoon tomato purée
1 teaspoon Worcestershire sauce
1 teaspoon salt
pepper
4 medium green peppers

In a saucepan gently fry the onion in the butter until softened but not browned. Remove the onion with a slotted spoon, reserving for later. Pour away any remaining fat and brown the mince in the pan. Add the onion, rice, herbs, purée, sauce and seasoning, mixing well together. Cut a shallow lid from the stalk end of each pepper and carefully scoop out the seeds, taking care not to cut through the outer wall. Fill the peppers with the meat mixture. Pour 300ml (½ pint) water into the pressure cooker and add the trivet. Stand the peppers on the trivet, ensuring that they won't fall over during cooking. Don't let them touch the wall of the pressure cooker, otherwise they will overcook at that point. Fit the lid and bring to pressure. Cook for 7 minutes at 15 lb (high) pressure. Reduce pressure quickly in cold water, taking care not to tip the pressure cookers, as the peppers could fall over and spill the filling.

STUFFED MARROW

Serves 4   *15 minutes at* 15 *lb* (*high*)

25g (1 oz) butter or margarine
4 rashers of streaky bacon, finely chopped
1 onion, finely chopped
100g (4 oz) mushrooms, finely chopped
1 tablespoon soy sauce

Stuffed Marrow contd.
1 teaspoon salt
pepper
pinch of thyme
100g (4 oz) cooked macaroni
1 medium sized marrow

In a pan gently fry the bacon in the butter until it starts to brown. Add the onion and fry gently until softened but not browned. Add the remaining filling ingredients, including the macaroni, mixing well together. Cool slightly while preparing the marrow. Peel the marrow and cut into 4 equal pieces. Cut away the centre pulp and seeds, leaving 4 marrow rings. Cut 4 squares of aluminium foil, large enough to wrap around each ring. Stand the rings on the foil and fill with the mixture. Seal the foil to form 4 parcels. Put 300ml (½ pint) water into the pressure cooker with the trivet and stand the parcels on the trivet. Fit the lid and bring to pressure. Cook for 15 minutes at 15 lb (high) pressure. Reduce pressure quickly in cold water. Remove the parcels from the pressure cooker and slide from the foil on to a serving dish.

PARSNIP SAVOURY

Serves 4   5 *minutes at* 15 *lb* (*high*)

700g (1½ lb) parsnips, sliced
salt and pepper
450g (1 lb) tomatoes, skinned and sliced
1 tablespoon parsley
100g (4 oz) grated cheese
300ml (½ pint) chicken stock

Divide the parsnips into three equal portions. Spread the first portion over the base of the pressure cooker, without the trivet. Season and cover with a layer of all the tomatoes. Sprinkle with parsley and cover with a second layer of parsnips. Season and sprinkle with all the cheese. Top with the final layer of parsnips. Season and pour over the stock. Fit the lid and bring to pressure. Cook for 5 minutes at 15 lb (high) pressure. Reduce pressure quickly in cold water.

CABBAGE ROLLS

Serves 4   6 *minutes at* 15 *lb* (*high*)

8 large green cabbage leaves
25g (1 oz) butter or margarine
1 onion, finely chopped
100g (4 oz) lambs liver, thinly sliced
225g (8 oz) long grain rice, cooked
a pinch of rosemary
1 teaspoon salt
pepper
298g (10½ oz) can condensed tomato soup
150ml (¼ pint) water

Remove from each leaf the white stalk, leaving a V-shaped cut. Plunge the leaves into a pan of salted boiling water and soak for 2 minutes. Drain and rinse. In a pan gently fry the onion in the butter until softened but not browned. Add the liver and quickly brown on all sides. Mix with the rice, rosemary and seasoning. Divide this mixture between the cabbage leaves and fold to form little parcels. Pour the condensed soup into the base of the pressure cooker, without the trivet, and stir in the water. Heat until mixed together. Place the rolls in the sauce, folded side downwards. Fit the lid and bring to pressure. Cook for 6 minutes at 15 lb (high) pressure. Reduce pressure quickly in cold water.

LEEK AND TOMATO CASSEROLE

Serves 4   3 *minutes at* 15 *lb* (*high*)

1kg (2 lb) leeks
227g (8 oz) can of tomatoes
2 tablespoons tomato purée
1 teaspoon salt
pepper
½ teaspoon mixed herbs
1 tablespoon lemon juice

Trim the dark green leaves from the leeks and save for flavouring soups and stews. Cut the white parts into 25mm (1 in) lengths. Put all the ingredients into the pressure cooker, without the trivet, fit the lid and bring to pressure. Cook for 3 minutes at 15 lb (high) pressure. Reduce pressure quickly in cold water.

7

RICE

Rice is a popular alternative to potatoes. It is convenient to use as it stores easily and doesn't need peeling!

Rice can be cooked either as a plain vegetable, to serve with curry or other oriental dishes, or together with vegetables, meat or fish as a complete dish. Apart from the following recipes, rice is an important ingredient of Kedgeree (page 73) and Chicken Risotto (page 59).

When pressure cooking rice as a separate vegetable, put 175g (6 oz) long grain rice into an unperforated basket or container. Add 550ml (1 pint) salted water and cover with greaseproof paper or aluminium foil. Put 300ml (½ pint) water into the pressure cooker, with the trivet and container, and bring to pressure. Cook for 5 minutes at 15 lb (high) pressure. Reduce pressure slowly at room temperature. Fluff the rice with a fork before serving.

LIVER RISOTTO

Serves 4   8 *minutes at* 15 *lb* (*high*)

25g (1 oz) butter or margarine
3 rashers streaky bacon, chopped
1 onion, chopped
225g (8 oz) lambs liver, sliced into thin strips
175g (6 oz) long grain rice
100g (4 oz) button mushrooms, quartered
550ml (1 pint) chicken stock
1 teaspoon salt
pepper

In the open pressure cooker, without the trivet, gently fry the bacon in the butter until starting to brown. Add the onion and fry until softened but not browned. Add the liver and brown quickly on all sides. Add the rice and stir fry for 2–3 minutes. Add the remaining ingredients and bring to the boil, stirring continuously. Reduce the heat to a medium setting, fit the lid and bring to pressure on that heat. Cook for 8 minutes at 15 lb (high) pressure. Reduce pressure slowly at room temperature. Remove the lid and continue to cook on a medium heat, fluffing up the grains of rice with a fork until separated.

RISOTTO ROMA

Serves 4   8 *minutes at* 15 *lb* (*high*)

25g (1 oz) butter or margarine
1 onion, chopped
1 clove garlic, crushed, optional
175g (6 oz) long grain rice
4 courgettes, thinly sliced
1 green pepper, de-seeded and chopped
550ml (1 pint) chicken stock

Risotto Roma contd.
1 tablespoon tomato purée
1 teaspoon salt
pepper
1 teaspoon dried mixed herbs

In the open pressure cooker, without the trivet, gently fry the onion and garlic in the butter until softened but not browned. Add the rice and stir fry for 2–3 minutes. Add all the remaining ingredients and bring to the boil, stirring continuously. Reduce the heat to a medium setting, fit the lid and bring to pressure. Cook for 8 minutes at 15 lb (high) pressure. Reduce pressure slowly at room temperature. Remove the lid and continue to cook on a low heat, fluffing up the grains of rice with a fork until separated.

RICE PUDDING

Serves 3–4   12 *minutes at* 15 *lb* (*high*)

25g (1 oz) butter or margarine
550ml (1 pint) milk
75g (3 oz) pudding rice
50g (2 oz) sugar
pinch ground nutmeg

Melt the butter or margarine in the pressure cooker, without the trivet, and swirl it round to coat the base. Add the milk and bring to the boil on a medium heat. Add the rice and sugar and stir until boiling again. Reduce the heat until the milk simmers gently. Fit the lid and bring slowly to pressure without increasing the heat. Cook for 12 minutes at 15 lb (high) pressure. Reduce pressure slowly at room temperature. Stir the pudding and, if wished, turn into an oven-proof dish, sprinkle with nutmeg and brown for a few minutes under the grill.

8

Although a pressure cooker is excellent for steaming puddings such as Mincemeat Roly Poly or All Fruits Pudding, it can also be used to cook more delicate desserts such as Crème Caramel and Stuffed Peaches.

This chapter includes a variety of steamed puddings, custards and fruit dishes, but if you wish to convert a favourite recipe to pressure cooking, follow these guidelines:

FRESH FRUIT

Ripeness and size

When selecting fruit for pressure cooking, remember that

for best results it should be roughly of equal size, with the same degree of ripeness. A small, ripe pear will fall apart before a larger, harder pear is cooked.

Purée

The trivet is not required when cooking fruit for a purée. In the open pressure cooker dissolve 100g (4 oz) sugar in the minimum recommended amount of water – 150ml ($\frac{1}{4}$ pint) or 300ml ($\frac{1}{2}$ pint).

Add the washed and roughly chopped fruit. As certain fruit tends to froth up during pressure cooking, do not fill more than half full.

Fit the lid and bring to pressure. Use 15 lb (high) for most fruit, the exception being rhubarb and apple which should be cooked at 10 lb (medium) pressure as it tends to froth during cooking. Refer to the table on page 100 for cooking times.

Reduce pressure slowly at room temperature.

Sieve the fruit or blend in a liquidizer. Use for pie fillings or add to cream or custard for fruit fool.

Soft fruit

The shape of more delicate soft fruit is best retained by cooking in a container. No liquid is added to the fruit and it produces its own, more concentrated juice. The container can be of metal, oven-proof glass or china or boilable plastic. A soufflé dish is ideal as it can be used afterwards for serving at the table.

Arrange the washed and prepared fruit in layers in the container. Sprinkle sugar, to taste, between each layer. Cover securely with greaseproof paper or aluminium foil.

Put into the pressure cooker 300ml ($\frac{1}{2}$ pint) water with a teaspoon of lemon juice. Stand the container on the trivet in the pressure cooker. Fit the lid and bring to 15 lb (high) pressure. Follow the table for cooking times, bearing in mind that a china or glass dish needs 4 minutes longer cooking time than a metal container. Reduce pressure quickly in cold water.

Stone fruit

When cooking stone fruits it is best to follow the method given for soft fruit. Either halve and stone the fruit or prick twice with a fork.

DRIED FRUIT

Wash the fruit in hot water and place in a bowl. Cover with boiling water. Allow 550ml (1 pint) for each 450g (1 lb) fruit. Cover and soak for 10 minutes.

Measure the soaking water and ensure that you have at least 300ml ($\frac{1}{2}$ pint) to pour into the pressure cooker, without the trivet. Add the fruit with 2–3 tablespoons sugar, to taste.

Fit the lid and bring to 15 lb (high) pressure. Follow the table for cooking times.

Allow pressure to reduce slowly at room temperature.

Cooking times at 15 lb (high) pressure for dried fruit

Apple rings	6 minutes
Apricots	4 minutes
Figs, pears, prunes	10 minutes
Peaches	5 minutes
Mixed fruit	10 minutes

STEAMED PUDDINGS

Container
The container used for steaming must be heat resistant. Use metal, boilable plastic, or oven-proof glass or china. Ensure that it is not too deep for your pressure cooker. Allow a gap of at least 5cm (2 in) between the top of the basin and the lid to allow steam to circulate.

Timing
The cooking times given in the recipes and in the adaptation table are for puddings in metal or boilable plastic. Increase the time by 10 minutes if using oven-proof glass or china.

Basic method
Grease the container and fill no more than three quarters to allow room for the pudding to rise.

Cover the container with greased aluminium foil or a double thickness of greased greaseproof paper. Ensure that this cover is securely tied down to prevent its rising up and blocking air vents.

Stand the container on the trivet in the pressure cooker and pour in the recommended amount of boiling water. Add a little lemon juice to the water to avoid the pressure cooker discolouring in hard water regions.

Fit the lid *without* the weight and heat until a thin jet of steam escapes from the vent. Reduce the heat so that the pudding steams gently for the recommended time, without the water boiling away furiously. It is during the steaming stage that the raising agent in the flour activates and the pudding rises.

Fit the weight and bring to 5 lb (low) pressure. Cook for the time recommended in the adaptation table. Reduce pressure slowly at room temperature to prevent the pudding from sinking. Remove the pudding using oven gloves.

Increased quantities

When increasing the quantities of a recipe, allow an extra 10 minutes cooking time for every additional 50g (2 oz) flour.

Tinned puddings

Tinned steamed puddings can be re-heated, unopened, in the pressure cooker. Stand on the trivet and add 300ml ($\frac{1}{2}$ pint) boiling water. Fit the lid and bring to pressure. Cook at 10 lb (medium) pressure for 20 minutes (large tin) or 10 minutes (small tin). Reduce pressure slowly.

Adaptation of steamed pudding recipes to pressure cooking

Normal cooking time	Water	Steaming	Pressure cooking at 5 *lb* (*low*)
30 mins	750ml (1$\frac{1}{2}$ pts)	5 mins	10 mins
1 hour	750ml (1$\frac{1}{2}$ pts)	15 mins	25 mins
2–3 hours	1 litre (2 pts)	20 mins	60 mins

Pressure cooking times for fresh fruit

		Purée mins.	Container method mins.
Apples, sliced	Purée at 10 lb (medium)	3	5–7
whole	See Stuffed Apples, page 104	–	–
Apricots, halved	Add 2 tbs water for container method	3	5–7
Blackcurrants		3	5–7

		Puree mins.	Container method mins.
Blackberries		3	5-7
Cherries	Cook whole with 2 tbs water for container method	–	5-7
Damsons	Add 2 tbs water for container method	3	5-7
Gooseberries		3	5-7
Greengages	Add 2 tbs water for container method	3	5-7
Loganberries		1	4-6
Pears	See Pears in Red Wine, page 103	3	–
Peaches, sliced **halved**	See Stuffed Peaches, page 105	3	5-7
Plums	Add 2 tbs water for container method	3	5-7
Raspberries		1	4-6
Rhubarb	Purée at 10 lb (medium)	1	5-7

EGG CUSTARD

Serves 4   10 *minutes at* 15 *lb* (*high*)

This is such an easy sweet to prepare. It is a good way of using up spare milk and an ingenious way of ensuring that children are getting their ration of milk.

425ml (¾ pint) milk
3 eggs
50g (2 oz) caster sugar
½ teaspoon vanilla essence
ground nutmeg

Grease a 550-ml (1-pint) pudding basin or soufflé dish. In a saucepan gently heat the milk to blood heat. In a bowl lightly whisk together the eggs, sugar and vanilla essence. Pour the hot milk over the egg mixture and stir well. Pour this custard mixture into the greased container. Sprinkle with a little nutmeg and cover securely with a circle of greaseproof paper or foil. Put the trivet into the pressure cooker with the basin on top. Pour in 300ml ($\frac{1}{2}$ pint) boiling water. Fit the lid and bring to pressure. Cook for 10 minutes at 15 lb (high) pressure. Reduce pressure slowly at room temperature. Remove the custard from the pressure cooker and allow to cool, if possible, overnight. It is best served chilled with fresh or poached fruit.

CRÈME CARAMEL

Serves 4–6   *Individual:* 3 *minutes at* 15 *lb* (*high*)
                          Large: 10 *minutes at* 15 *lb* (*high*)

This is the dinner party version of egg custard and is ideal to round off a rich meal. It can either be made in a large soufflé dish or in individual breakfast cups or dariole moulds.

Caramel:
4 tablespoons granulated sugar
4 tablespoons water

Custard:
425ml ($\frac{3}{4}$ pint) milk
3 eggs
$\frac{1}{2}$ teaspoon vanilla essence
50g (2 oz) caster sugar

Grease the mould(s). Put the sugar into a thick based saucepan and stand over a low heat. Stir with a wooden spoon until melted and caramel in colour. Remove the pan from the heat and add all the water. Do this quickly and with care as the mixture may spit. Stir again over a gentle heat until the water has boiled and dissolved the caramel. Pour into the mould(s) and swish around to coat the base.

Make up the custard using the same method as for Egg Custard (page 101), omitting the nutmeg, and pour into the mould(s). Cook in the same way, adjusting the time to the size of the mould. The individual moulds need 3 minutes and the large one 10 minutes at 15 lb (high) pressure. Reduce pressure slowly at room temperature. Cool and chill overnight. Run the blade of a knife around the sides and turn out on to a serving dish.

CHOCOLATE POTS

Serves 4   3 *minutes at* 15 *lb* (*high*)

These make a delightfully light finish to a dinner party.

100g (4 oz) Bournville chocolate
3 egg yolks
25g (1 oz) caster sugar
1 tablespoon rum or Cointreau
300ml ($\frac{1}{2}$ pint) milk
150ml ($\frac{1}{4}$ pint) double cream, whipped
1 tablespoon chocolate strands to decorate

Butter four individual porcelain baking dishes. Put a heat-resistant basin into a pan of hot water. Break the chocolate into the basin and leave for approximately 5 minutes until softened. Remove the basin from the pan and beat into the chocolate the egg yolks, sugar and rum or Cointreau. Mix together well. Heat the milk in a saucepan but do not allow to boil. Stir the milk into the chocolate mixture. Strain the mixture into a jug for easy pouring. Divide the mixture equally between the 4 baking dishes. Cover each one with greaseproof paper or foil. Put the trivet into the pressure cooker with 300ml ($\frac{1}{2}$ pint) water. Place the dishes on the trivet, ensuring that they don't touch the sides of the pressure cooker. If only three will fit in easily, cook the fourth one separately. Fit the lid and bring to pressure. Cook for 3 minutes at 15 lb (high) pressure. Reduce pressure slowly at room temperature. Cool the Chocolate Pots and chill. Serve decorated with whipped cream and chocolate strands.

PEARS IN RED WINE

Serves 4   8 *minutes at* 15 *lb* (*high*)

The cooking time will depend on the ripeness of the pears. If they are slightly over-ripe, reduce the time to 6 minutes.

4 large pears, well shaped and firm
50g (2 oz) caster sugar
300ml ($\frac{1}{2}$ pint) dry red wine
$\frac{1}{4}$ teaspoon cinammon
sliver of lemon peel

Peel the pears but take care to leave the stalk intact. Shave a slice off the bottom of each pear so that it will stand upright. Pour the wine into the pressure cooker, without the trivet, and add the sugar, cinammon and lemon peel. Dissolve the sugar over a low heat, stirring continuously. Stand the pears upright in the pressure cooker, ensuring that they don't touch the sides of the pressure cooker. Baste the pears with the liquid. Fit the lid and bring to pressure. Cook for 8 minutes at 15 lb (high) pressure. Reduce pressure quickly in cold water. Using a spoon lift the pears on to a serving dish. Don't lift them by the stalk as they could break off! If you intend serving the pears in a delicate cut-glass bowl, cool the wine mixture before pouring over the pears. Cool completely and chill before serving.

STUFFED APPLES

Serves 4   *4–6 minutes at* 15 *lb* (*high*)

4 cooking apples, washed and cored
50g (2 oz) sultanas
50g (2 oz) dried apricots, chopped
2 tablespoons honey
2 tablespoons soft brown sugar

Grease 4 squares of aluminium foil and stand an apple in the centre of each. Mix together the remaining ingredients and use to fill each apple. Crimp the foil at the edges to form a saucer shape. Put the trivet into the pressure cooker with 300ml ($\frac{1}{2}$ pint) water. Stand the apples and saucers on the trivet, ensuring that the apples don't touch the sides of the pressure cooker. Fit the lid and bring to pressure. Cook for 4–6 minutes at 15 lb (high) pressure. Reduce pressure quickly in cold water. Remove the apples and saucers to a serving dish and discard the foil.

APPLE DUMPLINGS

Serves 4   15 *minutes steaming*
                             20 *minutes at 5 lb (low)*

225g (8 oz) suet pastry (see Rhubarb and Orange Pudding, page 107)
4 medium cooking apples, peeled and cored
4 tablespoons mincemeat

Cut the pastry into 4 equal portions and roll each one into a circle large enough to wrap around one of the apples. Cut 4 squares of aluminium foil slightly larger. Stand an apple on each pastry circle and fill with the mincemeat. Moisten the edges of the pastry with water and fold over the apple, crimping the edges to seal. Stand a dumpling in each foil square and fold to form a sealed parcel. Stand the dumplings on the trivet in the pressure cooker. Pour in 550ml (1 pint) boiling water. Fit the lid *without* the weight and steam over a low heat for 15 minutes. Fit the weight and bring to pressure. Cook for 20 minutes at 5 lb (low) pressure. Reduce pressure slowly at room temperature. Serve with custard or cream.

STUFFED PEACHES

Serves 4   3 *minutes at 15 lb (high)*

300ml ($\frac{1}{2}$ pint) dry white wine
25g (1 oz) sugar
4 large, firm peaches
25g (1 oz) brown sugar
25g (1 oz) butter, melted
1 egg yolk
50g (2 oz) digestive biscuits, crushed
25g (1 oz) hazel nuts, chopped

In the open pressure cooker, without the trivet, dissolve the sugar in the wine over a low heat. Halve, stone and peel the peaches. Mix together the sugar and butter until well blended. Beat in the egg yolk and mix in the biscuit crumbs and nuts. Fill the peach halves with this mixture and stand them in the wine. Fit the lid and bring to pressure. Cook for 3 minutes at 15 lb (high) pressure. Reduce pressure quickly in cold water. Cool and serve chilled.

BREAD AND BUTTER PUDDING

Serves 2–3   6 *minutes at* 15 *lb* (*high*)

This everyday pudding can become something special if you
sprinkle the bread with a little liqueur, before cooking.
3 slices bread and butter, crusts removed
50g (2 oz) sultanas
1 large egg, beaten
300ml ($\frac{1}{2}$ pint) milk
25g (1 oz) caster sugar

Grease a 550ml (1 pint) pudding basin or heat-resistant
dish. Cut the bread into squares and arrange half over the
base of the dish, sprinkle with half the sultanas and top with
a second layer of each. Warm the milk to blood heat and
beat into the egg and sugar. Pour into the dish and cover
securely with greaseproof paper or aluminium foil. Put
300ml ($\frac{1}{2}$ pint) water into the pressure cooker with the trivet.
Stand the dish on the trivet, fit the lid and bring to pressure.
Cook for 6 minutes at 15 lb (high) pressure.

MINCEMEAT ROLY POLY

Serves 4–6   20 *minutes steaming*
                                       25 *minutes at* 5 *lb* (*low*)

225g (8 oz) suet pastry (see Rhubarb and Orange Pudding,
page 107)
280g (10 oz) mincemeat

Roll out the pastry on a lightly floured surface. Roll thinly
into an oblong which must not be wider than the diameter of
your pressure cooker. Dampen the edges with water and
spread the mincemeat over the pastry, leaving a narrow
margin on the four edges. Roll up from the short end and
crimp together the dampened edges. Wrap loosely in
aluminium foil, ensuring that it is sealed securely. Stand the
pudding on the trivet in the pressure cooker and pour in
850ml (1$\frac{1}{2}$ pints) boiling water. Fit the lid *without* the weight
and steam over a low heat for 20 minutes. Fit the weight and
bring to pressure. Cook for 25 minutes at 5 lb (low) pressure. Reduce pressure slowly at room temperature. Remove

the pudding carefully from the boiling water using two long-handled spoons. Unwrap the pudding and serve with custard or cream.

RHUBARB AND ORANGE PUDDING

Serves 4–6   20 *minutes steaming*
                     30 *minutes at* 5 *lb* (*low*)

225g (8 oz) self-raising flour
pinch of salt
100g (4 oz) shredded suet
6 tablespoons water
700g (1½ lb) rhubarb, in 25mm (1 in) pieces
grated rind of one orange
juice of one orange
175g (6 oz) brown sugar

Mix together the self-raising flour, salt and suet. With a fork mix in the cold water until a scone-like dough is achieved. Reserve one third for the lid of the pudding and roll the remainder into a circle on a lightly floured surface. Grease the inside of a 1 litre (2 pint) pudding basin and line with the suet pastry. Fill the basin with layers of rhubarb, each sprinkled with sugar and orange rind. Pour the orange juice over the rhubarb. Roll the remaining pastry to form the lid. Moisten the edges of the pastry with water, fit the pastry lid and crimp the edges. Cover with a circle of greased greaseproof paper or aluminium foil folded to allow the pudding to rise slightly. Make sure that this cover cannot become loose during cooking and block the air vent. Stand the basin on the trivet in the pressure cooker. Pour in 1½ litres (3 pints) boiling water. Fit the lid *without* the weight and steam over a low heat for 20 minutes. Fit the weight and bring to pressure. Cook for 30 minutes at 5 lb (low) pressure. Reduce pressure slowly at room temperature. Remove the basin from the pressure cooker and serve the pudding from the basin or turned out on to a serving dish.

ALL FRUITS PUDDING

Serves 6–8   20 *minutes steaming*
                          45 *minutes at 5 lb (low)*

100g (4 oz) butter
100g (4 oz) caster sugar
rind of 1 orange
juice of 1 orange
2 eggs
75g (3 oz) self-raising flour
50g (2 oz) breadcrumbs
100g (4 oz) mixed dried fruit, chopped (apricots, prunes,
    apples and pears)
50g (2 oz) glacé cherries
2 tablespoons Golden Syrup
4 rings tinned pineapple (thicken the juice with arrowroot to
    make a hot sauce)

Grease a 1-litre (2-pint) pudding basin. Cream together
the butter and sugar. Add the orange rind. Whisk the eggs
and add them to the creamed mixture. Mix together the
flour and breadcrumbs and fold into the pudding. Add the
orange juice. Halve two of the cherries, reserve for later and
chop the remainder. Mix in the cherries and dried fruit.
Spoon the syrup into the bottom of the basin. Arrange one
pineapple slice on the base and the remainder around the
sides. Put a half cherry in the centre of each. Pour the
mixture into the basin and cover with a circle of greased
greaseproof paper or aluminium foil, folded to allow the
pudding to rise slightly. Make sure that this cover cannot
become loose during cooking and block the air vent. Stand
the basin on the trivet in the pressure cooker. Fit the lid
without the weight and steam over a low heat for 20 minutes.
Fit the weight and bring to pressure. Cook for 45 minutes
at 5 lb (low) pressure. Reduce pressure slowly at room
temperature. Turn out of the basin to serve.

CHRISTMAS PUDDING

Makes 2 700g (1½ lb) puddings   20 *minutes steaming*
                               2 *hours at 15 lb (high)*

Make your Christmas Puddings at least 4–6 weeks before
Christmas to allow them to mature.

225g (8 oz) margarine, melted
200g (7 oz) flour
225g (8 oz) soft brown sugar
350g (12 oz) currants
225g (8 oz) raisins
175g (6 oz) sultanas
50g (2 oz) mixed peel
25g (1 oz) blanched almonds, chopped coarsely
25g (1 oz) glacé cherries, chopped
175g (6 oz) fresh breadcrumbs
grated rind 1 lemon
1 teaspoon nutmeg
1 tablespoon black treacle
2 large eggs
3 tablespoons milk
2 tablespoons rum

Mix all the ingredients together. Grease 2 550-ml (1-pint) pudding basins. Alternatively this mixture may be cooked in a 1-litre (2-pint) basin with cooking times given in the table below. Cover the puddings with a double layer of greased greaseproof paper. If your pressure cooker has insufficient room to cook both puddings together, cook one at a time. Stand the basin on the trivet in the pressure cooker. Pour in 1½ litres (3 pints) boiling water. Fit the lid *without* the weight and steam over a low heat for 20 minutes. Fit the weight and bring to pressure. Cook for 2 hours at 15 lb (high) pressure. Reduce pressure slowly at room temperature. When cold wrap in fresh greaseproof paper and store in a cool place until required.

Cooking and re-heating times for Christmas Pudding

Weight	Basin	Water	Steaming	Cooking	Re-heating
450g (1 lb)	550ml (1 pt)	1¼ litres (2½ pints)	15 mins	1¾ hours	20 mins
700g (1½ lb)	550ml (1 pt)	1½ litres (3 pints)	20 mins	2 hours	30 mins
1kg (2 lb)	1 litre (2 pts)	1¾ litres (3½ pints)	30 mins	3 hours	30 mins

CHOCOLATE SPONGE

Serves 4

20 minutes steaming
25 minutes at 5 lb (low)

50g (2 oz) butter or margarine
50g (2 oz) caster sugar
2 eggs, beaten
½ teaspoon vanilla essence
75g (3 oz) self-raising flour
1 tablespoon cocoa powder
milk

Grease a 500-ml (1-pint) pudding basin. Cream together the butter and the sugar until light and fluffy. Beat in the eggs and vanilla essence a little at a time. Sieve together the flour and cocoa and fold into the creamed mixture, adding sufficient milk to make a soft but firm consistency. Spoon the mixture into the basin and cover securely with a circle of greased greaseproof paper or aluminium foil. Stand on the trivet in the pressure cooker and pour in 850ml (1½ pints) boiling water. Fit the lid *without* the weight and steam over a low heat for 20 minutes. Fit the weight and bring to pressure. Cook for 25 minutes at 5 lb (low) pressure. Reduce pressure slowly at room temperature.

GOLDEN SUET PUDDING

Serves 4   20 *minutes steaming*
                         25 *minutes at 5 lb (low)*

100g (4 oz) self-raising flour
pinch of salt
50g (2 oz) caster sugar
50g (2 oz) shredded suet
1 egg, beaten
2 tablespoons milk
3 tablespoons golden syrup

Grease a 550-ml (1-pint) pudding basin. Mix flour and salt together and stir in the suet and sugar. Add the egg and milk and mix to a firm consistency. Spoon the golden syrup into the pudding basin and spoon the mixture on top. Cover securely with a circle of greased greaseproof paper or aluminium foil. Stand on the trivet in the pressure cooker and pour in 850ml (1½ pints) boiling water. Fit the lid *without* the weight and steam over a low heat for 20 minutes. Fit the weight and bring to pressure. Cook for 25 minutes at 5 lb (low) pressure. Reduce pressure slowly at room temperature.

9

COOKING FOR ONE

It sometimes happens that people living alone have limited cooking facilities, perhaps only a single ring in a bed-sitter. With such restrictions, it is tempting to resort to the frypan or to heating up canned concoctions, resulting in an unbalanced and rather expensive diet.

For a pensioner, bent on saving fuel costs, there is a danger that he or she may be reluctant to cook a complete meal as it would involve the use of one or two cooking rings, or even the oven.

In a pressure cooker a main course and vegetables can be cooked together, with a dessert included for good measure.

The secret is to choose food with similar cooking times or to adjust the preparation of food so that it cooks within the same time.

For example, meat can often be the deciding factor in calculating the cooking time. If a chop takes 10 minutes, the vegetables must be of the root variety which will not over-cook. Fish, on the other hand, takes less time and the potatoes have to be thinly sliced to cook within the time. Frozen peas need only a couple of minutes and are wrapped in foil to delay slightly their cooking.

I have assumed that anyone living alone has probably purchased a smaller size of pressure cooker, which generally has a recommended minimum level of liquid of 150ml (¼ pint).

If the manufacturer recommends a greater amount, you should increase accordingly the quantity specified in my recipes. This may mean that the amount of thickening at the end will have to be increased.

COTTAGE PIE and CARROTS
CINNAMON GOOSEBERRIES

7 minutes at 15 lb (high)

You will need the trivet, 2 perforated baskets and 1 un-perforated basket or basin.

175g (6 oz) mince
2 teaspoons dried onion flakes
½ beef stock cube
150ml (¼ pint) water
½ teaspoon salt
pepper
1 teaspoon Worcestershire sauce
2 medium potatoes, thinly sliced
4 carrots, sliced
100g (4 oz) gooseberries, topped and tailed
25g (1 oz) sugar
pinch of cinnamon
2 tablespoons water
1 tablespoon cornflour
1 tablespoon water

In the open pressure cooker, without the trivet, gently fry the mince, without adding any fat, until browned. Sprinkle over the onion and seasoning. Dissolve the stock cube in the water and pour into the pressure cooker. Place the trivet on top of the meat. Put the potatoes and carrots into the two baskets and season.

Butter the unperforated basket or basin and add the gooseberries. Mix together the sugar and cinnamon and sprinkle over the fruit. Add the water and cover with foil. Stand the three containers on the trivet and fit the lid. Bring to pressure and cook for 7 minutes at 15 lb (high) pressure. Reduce pressure quickly in cold water.

Remove the gooseberries and vegetables. Blend the cornflour with the water and pour over the meat. Bring to the boil stirring continuously until thickened. If a grill is available, the meat may be put into an oven-proof dish, covered with the sliced potatoes and browned. Alternatively, spoon the meat on to a plate, top with the potatoes and serve with the carrots dotted with butter.

LAMB CURRY with RICE
BAKED APPLE

10 minutes at 15 lb (high)

You will need the trivet, an unperforated basket or basin and a buttered square of aluminium foil.

2 teaspoons oil
2 lamb chops, excess fat trimmed
2 teaspoons curry powder
150ml ($\frac{1}{4}$ pint) water
$\frac{1}{2}$ stock cube
2 teaspoons dried onion flakes
25g (1 oz) sultanas
1 teaspoon chutney
1 tablespoon tomato purée
50g (2 oz) long grain rice
100ml (3 fluid oz) water, salted
1 cooking apple, cored
1 teaspoon brown sugar
1 teaspoon honey
2 teaspoons currants
1 tablespoon cornflour
1 tablespoon lemon juice

In the open pressure cooker, without the trivet, brown the lamb chops in the oil on both sides. Add the curry powder and stir fry for a couple of minutes. Dissolve the stock cube in the water and stir into the pressure cooker, adding sultanas, chutney, onion flakes and purée. Place the trivet on top of the meat. Put the rice into the unperforated basket and pour over the salted water. Cover securely with aluminium foil.

Score a ring around the centre of the apple. Stand it on the square of foil. Mix together the sugar, honey and currants, and fill the cavity. Fold the foil to form a parcel and seal securely. Stand the rice and apple on the trivet. Fit the lid and bring to pressure. Cook for 10 minutes at 15 lb (high) pressure. Reduce pressure quickly in cold water.

Remove the apple but leave covered with foil until ready to serve. Remove the container of rice but leave covered for the moment. Blend together the cornflour and lemon juice and pour into the pressure cooker. Bring to the boil, stirring continuously until thickened. Uncover the rice and fluff up with a fork to separate the grains. Spoon on to a serving dish and pour the curry over.

SAVOURY COD with PEAS and POTATOES EGG CUSTARD

8 minutes at 15 lb (high)

You will need the trivet, 2 greased squares of aluminium foil, a perforated separator basket and a large breakfast cup.

1 frozen portion cod steak
1 tomato, sliced
salt
pepper
pinch dried sage
50g (2 oz) frozen peas
knob of butter
2–3 potatoes, thinly sliced or diced
1 small egg, beaten
15g (½ oz) sugar
drop vanilla essence
150ml (¼ pint) milk
pinch of nutmeg

Place the cod on one of the foil squares and cover with the tomato slices. Season and sprinkle with dried sage. Fold the foil to form a sealed parcel. Put the peas on the second foil square, season and dot with the butter. Fold the foil into a parcel. Put the potatoes into the perforated separator basket and season.

Mix together the egg, sugar and vanilla essence. Add the milk, warmed if possible. Pour into the greased breakfast cup and sprinkle with nutmeg. Cover securely with aluminium foil. Put into the pressure cooker 150ml ($\frac{1}{4}$ pint) water with the trivet. Stand the perforated separator on the trivet and add the egg custard. Position the parcels of fish and peas around these two containers. Fit the lid and bring to pressure. Cook for 8 minutes at 15 lb (high) pressure. Reduce pressure slowly at room temperature.

Remove the egg custard and its foil cover. If wished, serve with sliced fresh fruit. Place the potatoes on a warmed serving plate and remove the fish and peas from their parcels.

ITALIAN PORK CHOP with POTATOES and PARSNIPS
CARIBBEAN BANANA

10 *minutes at* 15 *lb* (*high*)

You will need the trivet, two perforated separator baskets and a buttered square of aluminium foil.

1 tablespoon rum
25g (1 oz) raisins
1 pork chop
15g ($\frac{1}{2}$ oz) butter or margarine
2 teaspoons dried onions
2 teaspoons dried mixed peppers
227g (8 oz) can of tomatoes, including juice
salt
pepper
pinch of rosemary
2–3 potatoes, halved
3 parsnips, thickly sliced
1 banana, peeled
1 teaspoon Golden Syrup

Put the raisins into a cup and cover with the rum. Leave to soak while preparing the remainder of the meal. Trim the excess fat from the chop and brown in the butter on both sides in the pressure cooker, without the trivet. Add the dried onions and peppers, tomatoes, seasoning and rosemary. Put the potatoes and parsnips into the two separators and season. Place the trivet on top of the meat and stand the separators on the trivet.

Mould the aluminium foil into a hollow shape. Put the banana into the foil and pour over the syrup, raisins and rum. Fold over the foil to form a secure parcel and stand on the trivet. Fit the lid and bring to pressure. Cook for 10 minutes at 15 lb (high) pressure. Reduce pressure quickly in cold water.

Unwrap the banana carefully and serve in a bowl, covered with the sauce. Serve the potatoes and parsnips with the chop and spoon over the tomato sauce which may be thickened with cornflour if wished.

BEEF AND VEGETABLE CASSEROLE
BREAD AND BUTTER PUDDING

15 minutes at 15 lb (high)

You will need the trivet and a greased unperforated separator basket or small pudding basin.

15g ($\frac{1}{2}$ oz) lard
1 onion, chopped
175g (6 oz) stewing steak, cubed
2 potatoes, sliced
2 carrots, diced
1 parsnip, diced

(Sometimes these vegetables are sold together at supermarkets as individual 'stew packs'.)

salt
pepper
$\frac{1}{2}$ a stock cube, crumbled
150ml ($\frac{1}{4}$ pint) water
2 teaspoons Worcestershire sauce
2 slices of bread, buttered and cut into squares
2 teaspoons sultanas
1 teaspoon caster sugar
1 egg, beaten
150ml ($\frac{1}{4}$ pint) milk, warmed if possible
pinch of nutmeg

In the open pressure cooker, without the trivet, gently fry the onion in the lard until softened, but not browned. Add the steak and brown on all sides. Add the remaining vegetables, seasoning, stock cube and water and Worcestershire sauce. Place the trivet on top of the stew.

Arrange the bread and butter squares in layers with the sultanas and sugar in the basket or basin. Mix together the egg and milk and pour over the bread. Sprinkle with a pinch of nutmeg and cover securely with aluminium foil. Stand the container in the centre of the pressure cooker on the trivet. Fit the lid and bring to pressure. Cook for 15 minutes at 15 lb (high) pressure. Reduce pressure slowly at room temperature.

Remove the pudding which may be turned out on to a serving dish. The stew may be thickened using cornflour, if wished.

10

A pressure cooker can be used for making jam, marmalade, conserves or curds, or for bottling fruit.

When preparing jam, pressure cooking will speed up the softening stage and, as less liquid is used, the flavour is more concentrated and boiling to setting point is faster.

Not everybody owns a freezer to store fruit out of season and the only practicable alternative is to bottle. A pressure cooker offers a quicker and therefore cheaper alternative to oven bottling.

Jam making
The success of the jam depends on using good quality, undamaged fruit. Berry fruits such as raspberries and straw-

berries do not require softening under pressure but the open pressure cooker may be used as a large pan to prepare the jam in the traditional way.

The trivet is not used.

The softening stage releases the pectin from the fruit so that the jam will eventually set. Put the water and fruit into the pressure cooker, ensuring that it is no more than half full. Fit the lid and bring to 10 lb (medium) pressure. The fruit should be cooked for up to 5 minutes, depending on the ripeness of the fruit and its type. Allow pressure to reduce slowly at room temperature.

Put the clean dry jam-jars to warm in a low oven.

Calculate the amount of sugar required. This will be approximately equal to the weight of the fruit. Warm the sugar slightly in a bowl in a low oven as this improves the colour and flavour.

Add the sugar and cook over a low heat, stirring continuously until dissolved. Do not fit the lid after the sugar has been added.

Bring to the boil and boil rapidly until the jam reaches setting point. You can gauge this most accurately with a sugar thermometer as setting occurs at 104°C (221°F). Alternatively stir the jam with a wooden spoon, cool the spoon slightly and if the jam partly jells, setting point has been reached. A third method is to remove the pressure cooker from the heat and spoon a little jam on to a cold saucer. Leave it to cool then rub your finger over the surface. If it wrinkles the jam has set.

As soon as the jam reaches setting point remove the pressure cooker from the heat. Remove any scum and ladle the jam into a Pyrex jug. I find it easier to pour the jam into the jars rather than use a ladle. Stand the jars on newspaper to prevent their cracking. Cover with waxed discs and, when cool, cover with cellophane and label.

APRICOT JAM

Approx 2¼kg (5lb)　　　　　　10 *minutes at* 15 *lb (high)*

450g (1 lb) dried apricots, washed and chopped
1 litre (2 pints) boiling water
juice 1 lemon
1·5kg (3 lb) sugar

Put the apricots into the pressure cooker without the trivet. Cover with boiling water and leave to soak for 10 minutes. Add the lemon juice, fit the lid and bring to pressure. Cook for 10 minutes at 15 lb (high) pressure. Reduce pressure slowly at room temperature. Add the sugar and boil over a low heat until dissolved. Boil rapidly until the jam reaches setting point. Skim if necessary. Cool the jam slightly until a skin forms to prevent the fruit rising in the jars. Pour into warmed, dry jars and cover with waxed discs. Cover with cellophane or lids when cold.

DAMSON JAM

Approx 2¼*kg* (5 *lb*)   5 *minutes at* 10 *lb* (*medium*)

1·25kg (2½ lb) damsons, washed
300ml (½ pint) water
1·5kg (3 lb) sugar

Put the damsons and water into the pressure cooker without the trivet. Fit the lid and bring to pressure. Cook for 5 minutes at 10 lb (medium) pressure. Reduce pressure slowly at room temperature and complete the method as for Apricot Jam.

ORANGE MARMALADE

Approx 2¼*kg* (5 *lb*)   10–15 *minutes at* 15 *lb* (*high*)

700g (1½ lb) Seville oranges, washed and halved
juice of 1 large or 2 small lemons
550ml (1 pint) water
1·5kg (3 lb) sugar

Squeeze the juice from the oranges and tie the pith and pips in a muslin pouch. Cut the peel as thinly as preferred. Soak the peel and pouch of pips in water overnight. Put the orange and lemon juice, water, peel and pips into the presure cooker, without the trivet, fit the lid and bring to pressure. Cook at 15 lb (high) pressure for 10–15 minutes according to the thickness of the peel. Reduce pressure slowly at room temperature. When the mixtu re has cooled squeeze juice from the muslin pouch into the pressure cooker then discard the pouch. Add the sugar and bring to the boil over a low heat until dissolved. Boil rapidly until the marmalade reaches setting point. Skim and continue as for Apricot Jam (page 119).

GOOSEBERRY AND GINGER JAM

Approx 2¼*kg* (5*lb*)   3 *minutes at* 10 *lb* (*medium*)

1·5kg (3 lb) gooseberries, topped and tailed
50g (2 oz) crystallized ginger, chopped
300ml (½ pint) water
1·5kg (3 lb) sugar

Put the gooseberries, ginger and water into the pressure cooker without the trivet. Fit the lid and bring to pressure. Cook for 3 minutes at 10 lb (medium) pressure. Reduce pressure slowly at room temperature and complete the method as for Apricot Jam (page 119).

APPLE JELLY

3 *minutes at* 10 *lb* (*medium*)

1·5kg (3 lb) cooking apples, washed
juice of one lemon
300ml (½ pint) water
sugar

Remove any bruised parts of the apples. Slice thickly without peeling or removing the core. Put the apple, lemon juice and water into the pressure cooker without the trivet. Fit the lid and bring to pressure. Cook for 3 minutes at 10 lb (medium) pressure. Reduce pressure slowly at room temperature. Mash the fruit and strain it through a jelly bag or clean tea towel into a bowl. Don't squeeze the bag to speed up the process as this will make the jelly cloudy. Measure the liquid and weigh 450g (1 lb) sugar for each 550ml (1 pint) juice. Return the juice to the clean pressure cooker and add the sugar. Bring to the boil over a low heat to dissolve the sugar and boil in the open pan until the jelly reaches setting point. Pour into dry, warmed jars and cover each with a waxed disc. Cover with cellophane or lids when cold.

REDCURRANT JELLY

1 *minute at* 10 *lb* (*medium*)

1·5kg (3 lb) redcurrants, washed
300ml (½ pint) water
sugar

Don't remove the stalks from the fruit. Put the red-currants and water into the pressure cooker without the trivet. Prepare in the same way as for Apple Jelly (page 121), allowing 550g (1¼ lb) sugar for each 550ml (1 pint) liquid.

LEMON CURD

10 *minutes at* 15 *lb* (*high*)

4 eggs, beaten
450g (1 lb) caster sugar
grated rind of 4 lemons
strained juice of 2 lemons
75g (3 oz) butter, cubed

Strain the eggs into a heat-resistant bowl and mix in the sugar. Add the lemon rind, juice and butter. Cover securely with a circle of greased greaseproof paper. Pour 300ml (½ pint) water into the pressure cooker with the trivet. Stand the bowl on the trivet. Fit the lid and bring to pressure. Cook for 10 minutes at 15 lb (high) pressure. Reduce pressure slowly at room temperature. Remove the basin from the pressure cooker and stir with a wooden spoon until well blended. Pour into dry, warmed jars and cover with a waxed disc. When cold cover with cellophane or lids. Store in a cool place and use within 6 weeks.

GREEN TOMATO CHUTNEY

Approx 1½*kg* (3 *lb*)   10 *minutes at* 15 *lb* (*high*)

425ml (¾ pint) vinegar
1·5kg (3 lb) green tomatoes, thinly sliced
3 onions, finely chopped

3 cooking apples, peeled, cored and finely chopped
175g (6 oz) sultanas
2 teaspoons salt
3 teaspoons pickling spice tied in a muslin pouch
250g (9 oz) soft brown sugar

Put half the vinegar into the pressure cooker without the trivet. Add the remaining ingredients except for the sugar. Fit the lid and bring to pressure. Cook for 10 minutes at 15 lb (high) pressure. Reduce pressure quickly in cold water. Add the remaining vinegar and the sugar. Bring to the boil in the open pan and simmer over a low heat until the chutney thickens. Remove the spices and pour the chutney into dry, warmed jars. Cover immediately with a waxed disc and plastic lid. If the jars are fitted with metal lids, ensure they are lacquered or fitted with a cardboard lining, otherwise the acid in vinegar will attack the metal.

APPLE CHUTNEY

Approx 1·8kg (4 lb)   12 *minutes at* 10 lb (*medium*)

300ml (½ pint) malt vinegar
1·5kg (3 lb) cooking apples, peeled, cored and diced
450g (1 lb) onions, finely chopped
225g (8 oz) sultanas
1 teaspoon salt
pinch cayenne pepper
700g (1½ lb) brown sugar

Put the vinegar into the pressure cooker without the trivet. Add the remaining ingredients except for the sugar. Fit the lid and bring to pressure. Cook for 12 minutes at 10 lb (medium) pressure. Reduce pressure quickly in cold water. Add the sugar and bring to the boil in the open pan, simmering until thickened. Store as for Green Tomato Chutney.

Fruit bottling
Choose firm, unblemished fruits of equal size and ripeness to ensure even cooking. Fruit such as apple, which discolours when peeled, should be covered in a solution of 1 teaspoon salt to 550ml (1 pint) water until ready for bottling. Rinse well in cold water before packing the apple into the bottles.

Hard fruit such as apples and pears need slight cooking before bottling. Put 300ml ($\frac{1}{2}$ pint) water into the pressure cooker with the trivet and pile the fruit on the trivet, ensuring that the pressure cooker is no more than half full. Fit the lid and bring to 15 lb (high) pressure. Reduce pressure immediately in cold water to avoid overcooking.

As soft fruit such as raspberries and strawberries tend to shrink when cooked, it is best to soak them overnight in a heavy syrup before bottling.

Fruit bottled in a syrup will give better results in terms of flavour and colour but water may be used instead. When making the syrup boil granulated sugar in water for about a minute. If you prefer a light syrup use 50–100g (2–4 oz) sugar for each 550ml (1 pint) water. For a heavier syrup for desserts, use 175–225g (6–8 oz) sugar for each 550ml (1 pint) water. 5 lb (low) pressure is used when bottling fruit.

Method

Immerse the clean jars and lids in boiling water while preparing the fruit.

Pack the cleaned fruit into the jars. Pack tightly to the shoulder of the jar.

Bring to the boil the prepared syrup and, using a jug, pour into the jars, a little at a time, releasing any air bubbles by tapping the jar gently against a board. Leave a space at the top of about 5mm ($\frac{1}{4}$ inch).

Fit the rubber bands and tops. If the jars are sealed by metal clips these should be fitted at this stage, but if metal screw bands are used they should be screwed down until tight then unscrewed for a quarter turn. This is to allow air and steam to escape from the jars during bottling. Return the jars to the hot water.

Put the trivet into the pressure cooker upside down and pour in 1 litre (2 pints) boiling water. Stand the jars in the pressure cooker ensuring that they don't touch each other or the sides of the pressure cooker, otherwise they could crack during processing.

Using a medium heat bring to 5 lb (low) pressure and cook for the recommended time given in the table below. Reduce pressure slowly at room temperature.

Remove the jars and screw tight the jars fitted with metal screw bands. Metal clips tighten automatically.

Test the seal the next day by unscrewing the bands or

removing the clips. If the covers remain firmly in position, label the jars and store. If they can be removed, the fruit should be used as soon as possible and you should examine the bottle, cover, seal and band or clip as one of them could be faulty.

Fruit	*Minutes at 5 lb (low)*
Apple, thickly sliced	1
Apricots, halved and stoned	1
Blackberries	1
Cherries	1
Damsons	1
Gooseberries (only when firm)	1
Greengages	1
Loganberries	3
Peaches, skinned and halved	3
skinned and sliced	1
Pears, halved or quartered	3
Pineapple, cubed	3
Plums, whole or halved	1
Raspberries	1
Rhubarb	2
Strawberries	3

Index